ACCOUNTING

FOR

GENERAL MEDICAL

PRACTITIONERS

A *Practical Approach*

M. Bashir Khatri BA (Hons) Acc.

Richard C Pennack FCCA

First published 1998
By PKA Books Limited, 71 Beaumanor Road, Leicester, LE4 5QD

© Copyright 1998 M. Bashir Khatri and Richard C Pennack

Crown copyright is reproduced with the permission of the Controller of Her
Majesty's Stationery Office.

ISBN: 0 9534516 0 7

A catalogue record for this book is available from the British Library.

Important Disclaimer

No responsibility for loss occasioned to any person acting or refraining from action as
a result of any material in this publication can be accepted by the authors or
publishers.

Readers entering into transactions on the basis of such information should seek the
services of a competent professional adviser as this publication is sold on the understanding that the publisher is not engaged in rendering legal or accounting advice or
other professional services. The publisher and the authors expressly disclaim all and
any liability and responsibility to any person, whether a purchaser or reader of this
publication or not, in respect of anything and of the consequences of anything, done or
omitted to be done by any such person in reliance, whether wholly or partially, upon
the whole or any part of the contents of this publication.

The publisher advises that any materials issued by other bodies and reproduced in this
publication are not the authorised official versions of those materials. In their
preparation, however, the greatest care has been taken to ensure exact conformity with
the material as issued.

The names of the persons and places in the publication are purely fictional and any
resemblance to actual or dead is purely coincidental.

Printed by Print Logistics, Leicester.
Typeset in Times Roman.

Table of Contents

Dedication

To my son, Atif, who is a very gentle and affectionate child - a very special child, who, sadly, suffers from Williams Syndrome, which is non hereditary, and a rare medical condition.

MBK

The Williams Syndrome Foundation.

For information about WS, please contact:

> The Williams Syndrome Foundation Limited
> 161 High Street
> Tunbridge
> Kent
> TN9 1BX
>
> Registered Charity No: 281014
>
> Tel: 01732 365152
> Fax: 01732 360178
> Website Address: http://www.williams-syndrome.org.uk

Acknowledgement

The authors would like to thank each other for their mutual support during the writing of this book and further acknowledge the help of their secretary, Val Bailey.

Their acknowledgements are due to Liz Densley who has read their manuscript and made valuable suggestions.

Special thanks go to their wives and children for their patience and tolerance.

Note to the reader:
In the interest of clarity masculine form has been used throughout the book.

Preface

This book focuses on the accountancy side of the General Medical Practice. Our aim is to meet the needs of general medical practitioners and their business managers who want to understand 'accounting' in a practical way. It is not written in the style of a textbook but as a fictional case study that encapsulates a 'real' situation of a partnership and gives an insight into the financial control of the general practice. The purpose of the book is to give the reader a clear understanding on the role played by a business manager.

As the title suggests, Accounting for General Medical Practitioners, a practical approach, the book is a general-purpose exposition of accounting and we hope that our readers will find the contents of the book easy to follow and comprehend. Concise explanation of the fees and allowances are extracted from the Red Book together with the latest figures. Detailed preparation and presentation of the financial and management accounts are provided together with the tax implication to the case study.

The reader should treat this book as a guide; always check with appropriate authorities if in doubt. Always seek advice from specialists on accountancy and tax matters.

We hope that the book will make a useful work of reference to business managers in general medical practice.

M. Bashir Khatri

Richard C Pennack   December 1998

Foreword

The accountancy side of General Medical Practice is often a mystery to GPs and their business and practice managers. The depth of information contained in this book will be interesting to the most demanding of business managers whilst it is set out in an interesting enough format for the least interested practice managers to be able to benefit from it as well.

As an accountant specialising in dealing with medical practitioners, I spend a lot of my time explaining what goes into a set of accounts, what various terms in the financial statements mean and what statistics might be meaningful. A publication such as this will help both GPs and managers alike to understand. This will not only make my job easier, it will make the management of the practice finances that much more efficient.

As stated in the preface, a book such as this should be treated as a guide; not everything mentioned in the book will apply to all practices and specialist advice will still be needed, but it will be a useful addition to any practice's library.

LIZ DENSLEY
Honey Barrett Chartered Accountants
Secretary and founder member of **aisma**
(The Association of Independent Specialist Medical Accountants)
Tel: 01424 730345
E-mail: aisma@honeybarrett.co.uk   December 1998

Chapter 1

Introduction

General Medical Practices

*The Role of a Business Manager
in General Practice*

*Safeguard the Assets
of the Medical Practice*

Introduction

General Medical Practitioners (GPs) are independent contractors to the National Health Service (NHS) and, therefore, they are regarded as self-employed medical practitioners. They need to be much more than healthcare providers. They must have a business-like approach in operating their medical practices. This involves the understanding of finance and accountancy.

Medical practices receive their income from the Health Authority (HA) as laid down in the Statement of Fees and Allowances payable to GPs in England & Wales, in other words, the 'Red Book'. This is published by the Department of Health and provides detailed guidance on GP finances. The 'grossing up' principle should be applied and adhered to when presenting the practice accounts. This means that where a HA meets a revenue expense directly, or indirectly, the maximum amount is shown for expense rather than netting off expenses against reimbursements. This helps the Review Body to assess GPs' Cost-Plus Contract more accurately.

GPs may also receive non-NHS income in the form of private patients' fees, cremation fees, insurance examinations, and the like. It is important that all income received of a medical nature, from whatever source, should be disclosed in the accounts.

The GPs have responsibility of managing their practices and this requires decision making. Information is the key to decision making. Proper accounting systems, therefore, produce vital information for:

- day to day control of the practice,
- allocation of profits amongst partners;
- running the practice most economically and efficiently,
- compliance with the new tax regulations - 'self-assessment' introduced by the Finance Act 1994.

General Medical Practices (GMPs)

The 1998 Review Body report indicated that around 2430 GPs, 8% of the GPs in the country, practice as sole practitioners. The rest practice in partnerships as follows:

No. of partners	% of GPs
2 - 3	26%
4 - 5	35%
6 - 10	29%
10 +	2%

Single handed (sole) practitioners and partnership explained

A sole practitioner is a sole owner, in total control of his practice, and is responsible to himself. The success of his practice depends on his efforts and he enjoys flexibility. He makes decisions without hindrance and with minimum of delay. However, there are disadvantages of running a practice as a sole practitioner. The practice success is limited to what he can achieve by his own ability, and there may be a shortfall in some areas such as shortage of capital or expertise.

The other option is to run a practice with someone else and form a partnership. There are certain legal implications in this case.

Nature of partnership: Sec: 1 of the Partnership Act, 1890 defines partnership as 'the relationship which subsists between persons carrying on a business in common with a view of profit'. A partnership may be created by verbal or written agreement. It may also imply from the conduct of the parties. In practice, most firms have a formal agreement or 'partnership deed' which will cover all aspects of the partnership and in general they will cover the following matters:

(a) Capital - It should properly define whether partners have a share of property capital, fixed capital, and/or current capital.

(b) Interest on Capital and Drawings - It should specify whether interest is receivable and/or payable and at what rate.

(c) Division of profits - It should clarify the sharing of the practice profits amongst partners. A junior doctor may have an arrangement with his senior colleagues on fixed share minimum and he will still be regarded as a partner. A GP has to exhibit all the characteristics of a partner in the practice to qualify for a basic practice allowance. If he fails to do that, then the basic practice allowance can be withdrawn by the HA.

(d) Partnership Income - The firm will receive its income from HA in the form of fees, allowances, and reimbursement of expenses as well as non-NHS income. A problem arises when a partner receives income from an outside appointment that is subject to tax and National Insurance Contributions (NIC). To overcome this problem, the partner should apply for Nil Tax (NT) coding and NIC postponement as the income will form a part of the partnership income and will be assessed under Schedule D.

(e) Partnership and personal expenses - All expenses related to running the practice and paid out of partnership funds are charged to Profit and Loss account. There is no problem on these partnership expenses. However, a problem arises when each partner's personal expenses are included such as car running expenses, wife's salary and pension, private telephone, medical subscriptions, study allowance and so on. These expenses could have been paid by the practice or by each partner personally This will depend upon the firm's own policy and should be covered in the partnership deed.

(f) Accounts preparation - The partnership deed should stipulate that the accounts shall be prepared once a year. The accounts produced shall be binding on the partners once they approve them.

(g) Goodwill - Goodwill in NHS general medical practices was made illegal in 1948. There is a statutory prohibition laid down by the NHS Act 1977. However, goodwill of a private practice could be valued and sold.

(h) Retirement/death - The deed should specify the terms on the retirement or death of a partner.

In the absence of a formal agreement, the Partnership Act, 1890 provides for:

(a) an equal share of capital, profits and losses;

(b) the firm to indemnify a partner for payments made by him on behalf of the partnership business;

(c) no interest on capital as such, except interest at 5% per annum on a partner's advances beyond the amount of a partner's agreed capital;

(d) majority decision be seen to rule where differences of opinions are expressed in ordinary matters;

(e) unanimous consent of all partners where any decision changes the nature of the partnership or the terms of agreement such as the introduction of a new partner;

(f) the partnership books to be maintained at the office of the partnership and all the partners to have access to them on request.

Practice liability:

A sole practitioner is personally liable for all the debts of his practice. The same applies to the partners in the firm. This means that the actions of one partner binds both the firm and all the other partners jointly and severally.

Dissolution:

A partnership ceases by agreement of all the partners; on the retirement of a partner; or on bankruptcy of a partner; or on the death of a partner; or by Court Order.

The role of a business manager in general medical practice

A business manager is regarded as an information manager. He is responsible for providing information both within the practice and to third parties. He plays a role of financial controller in addition to the administration of the practice. He ensures that proper information systems are in operation and tries to avoid potential problems such as poor liquidity and deficiency of cost controls. He reports to the partners on the present and future financial position. His responsibilities include:

(a) General administration:
Day to day management of the practice
Delegate work to staff
Deals with HA in relation to statements of fees and allowances
Ensure accuracy of all claim procedures and timely payment of bills
Working in close relationship with the practice manager who is responsible on the clinical side of the practice.
Represent the practice at meetings with the HA and other parties.

(b) Financial accounting:
Maintaining an accurate record of practice income and expenditure.
Preparing bank reconciliation and cash control periodically.
Producing financial statements for the practice accountant annually.

(c) Cost and management accounting:
Producing management accounts periodically
Reporting on cost controls and maximisation of contributions
Preparing budgets for the practice
Preparing projections of cash flow as well as Income Statement
Evaluation of the management efficiency of the practice

(d) Payroll management
Administrative processes involved in payroll preparation.
Liaising with the practice manager in appointment of staff, claims and reimbursements of staff wages from HA.

(e) Stock control
Liaising with the practice manager to oversee the stock control system
Ensuring an accurate balance is kept of purchases against items dispensed

(f) Business planning:
Maintaining and updating the practice business plan

(g) Computer system management:
Delegating and supervising work carried out by computer personnel.
Ensuring the quality and accuracy of data capture.
Maintaining appropriate back up systems.

Safeguard the assets of the medical practice

The assets of the medical practice have to be protected and having a proper internal control system does this. Internal control means the whole system of control, financial and otherwise, established by the partners in the efficient running of the practice. However, most GPs do not favour internal control because they consider their organisations to be too small and their employees work on trust in an informal environment. They feel that the cost of internal control to be too high to implement. Well, there is a problem here but this does not mean that internal control should be ignored. There are ways of implementing controls over the recording of transactions and maintenance of assets even where the number of staff is small.

The measures that can be used are:

(a) The use of controlled pre-numbered forms. This system helps to trace and verify transactions. Any gaps in the numerical sequence have to be investigated. All void copies of documents should be kept.

(b) When an invoice is paid, mark on the face of the document with cash or cheque number, amount paid and dates when it was paid. It helps to trace and verify the transaction.

(c) Match and verify the information on the purchase order to the information on the invoice. Investigate any discrepancies.

(d) Once the document has been matched and cheques signed, the document should not be returned to the person who prepared it. This prevents any changes to the document after it has been approved and signed.

(e) With larger practices, two signatures on a cheque is a good control. These signatories should be the partners or a partner and a manager. A manager should be allowed to sign a cheque for a small amount, say, up to £250.

(f) When purchasing equipment, obtain written bids, with pricing, for such purchases.

(g) All major purchases of the practice should be validated with a pre numbered order document.

(h) Segregation of duties - no one person should be responsible for the recording and processing of a complete transaction.

(i) Promptness of recording transactions is important. Delay can create problems.

(j) Access to computers should be restricted by means of passwords. Also, access to medical supplies should be restricted to authorised personnel only.

(k) Reconcile actual stock to inventory records and cash book to bank statements periodically.

(l) A register of fixed assets should be maintained and checked.

(m) Aged debtor and aged creditor balances reports should be examined by the partner. Any write off should be authorised by the partner responsible.

(n) Budgetary control enables practices to review from time to time the progress of their activities. Actual and budgeted figures are compared. Any variances should be investigated.

Chapter 2

The Case Study:
The East Road Surgery

The Case Study: The East Road Surgery

In January 1994, Dr Brayne and Dr Drane met at the Practitioners' Seminar where they discussed the prospects of establishing a general medical practice. Both of them qualified at the Leicester University in 1980. Dr Brayne specialised in paediatrics, dermatology, asthma, diabetes and minor surgery. He worked in hospitals and health-care centres for a number of years. Dr Drane specialised in gynaecology, hormone replacement therapy and women's health. She worked in hospitals too, and did locums for local general medical practices. Both doctors sought professional advice and were made aware of all pros and cons of setting up a practice.

Drs Brayne and Drane opted for a partnership venture. They commenced a new equal partnership practice on 1 April 1994 after applying to the Health Authority. They were given permission to set up in response to local population growth. The partnership agreement, which covered all aspects of the partnership, was signed. They introduced £30,000 in cash as capital. They acquired a freehold property for £155,000 that was borrowed on 25 years mortgage at around 1.25% above base rate from the bank. They incurred capital expenditures as follows:

£7,250 on furniture, fixtures and fittings, £8,500 for the cost of purchasing and installing a computer system for the use of the practice and £9,750 for office and medical equipment. 50% of the costs of computer equipment were reimbursed by the HA. The bank provided an overdraft facility for up to £15,000.

In the year ending 31 March 1997, the practice refurbished and extended its premises costing £52,800 of which £17,600 was received as a grant towards providing facilities for disabled people from the Health Authority. Fixtures and fittings cost £6,600. £28,600 was borrowed over 22 years by re mortgaging the property on the same terms and from the same lender. Further furniture, medical and computer equipment were purchased for £30,755, including £3,990 HP interest, paying a deposit of £5,500 and the balance was financed by hire purchase over 24 equal instalments. The furniture cost £7,965 and the medical equipment cost £7,800. The computer equipment was an upgrade costing £11,000 of which 50% was reimbursed under the GP computer scheme. The firm was leasing office equipment and paying £200 per quarter that expired at the end of 31 March 1998.

The bookkeeper prepared the closing balances for the year ended 31 March 1997 and passed it over to the professional firm of accountants. The accountants scrutinised the balances and amended the figures before preparing the financial statements. They prepared the journals, which were then passed over to the surgery to process through and bring forward the correct balances. The trial balance as at 1 April 1997 was extracted and is shown in chapter 3.

At the beginning of the current financial year, 6 April 1997, a new partner, Dr Payne was introduced by acquiring 1/3rd of the value of all the partnership assets. The net assets of the partnership were valued at £90,000. Prior to becoming a partner, Dr Payne was a sole practitioner and his surgery was only a hundred yards away from the East Road Surgery. His surgery premises were on rent for 12 months and on the date of expiry he worked out a partnership arrangement with Drs Brayne and Drane to take effect from the day the lease expired. He specialised in orthopaedics, psychiatry, care of the elderly, child health and minor surgery. He brought a couple of staff and all his 1498 patients with him, increasing the partnership practice to just over 8000 patients.

Dr Brayne and Dr Drane had now been in partnership for 3 years and the practice was growing fast. The partners were very ambitious and wanted to develop the practice into a modern healthcare centre. They approached a management consultant who advised them that there was a need for an information manager, who will run the practice in a business-like manner. Presently, they employed part time staff to do the bookkeeping and this was not enough. Both agreed and asked the consultant to assist in appointing an appropriate information manager.

Applications were received and short-listed. Interviews were held and notes were made of each candidate's performance. A suitable candidate, S Patel, emerged from the selection process. He was an accountancy graduate and had worked within the accountancy profession for a number of years. He had been involved in dealing with clients who were GPs and this is how he developed his interest in medical practices. The last firm of chartered accountants he worked for was also a member of AISMA. Patel was very enthusiastic and this impressed both Dr Brayne and Dr Drane. The partners felt that although Patel did not fully meet the job specifications, he had the ability to manage and grow with the firm. Hence, he was offered the position of a business manager at a commencing salary of £24,000 and a good annual review. He immediately accepted the offer.

The first task of the business manager was to review the systems of internal control of East Road Surgery. He wanted to know how reliable was the data produced by the present information system. He felt that good decisions couldn't be made on unreliable data. His idea was to design and implement an effective and flexible system of internal control, which would fit in a small business environment. He observed and noted the problems and reported to the partners.

As part of the internal control, the business manager organised a register of fixed assets. The register contained - date of purchase, supplier's name, cost, grant received, current valuation, insurance cover, location, depreciation rate, leased or on hire purchase, any improvements or maintenance required and so on. Such information was useful because it provided a link between the accounts and the fixed assets, a record for tax purposes and a record in case of insurance claim.

Mortgage repayment and interest schedule was also prepared.

The partnership practice employed a full time assistant, Dr Zain who specialised in preventive medicines, menopause, hormone replacement and vasectomies. He had been offered a partnership on a fixed salary as from 6 April 1998. It should be noted that the NHS would recognise Dr Zain as a partner on the condition that he is a full time practitioner and his share of the partnership profit was at least one-third of the partner with the largest share.

Due to the population growth in the area, it is expected that the numbers of patients are to increase by around 10% in the following year. The diverse expertise of the GPs is also attracting more and more patients. The practice has undergone considerable change and development since 1994. The partners want to offer an extensive and growing range of services to their patients and therefore further developments have been planned. The firm has employed an experienced business manager to administer and report to the partners. Other ancillary staff includes a practice manager, three practice nurses, two receptionists and a secretary/data processing clerk, a community nurse who offers community nursing advice and a midwife who attends to ante natal care. The practice places a high emphasis on teamwork in health care.

The practice ought to comply with the law in relation to the employment of staff. The partners should be aware of their rights and duties as employers. The employee must be given a written statement of the conditions and terms of employment. The employment law is very complex and there are various agencies, which should be contacted for advice and guidance. These agencies are Advisory, Conciliation & Arbitration Service, Commission for Racial Equality, Equal Opportunity Commission, Inland Revenue and Department of Trade & Industry.

Here, we presume that the East Road surgery is implementing the requirements of the employment law. The PAYE scheme is dealt with in the chapter on taxation.

Further information was available as follows:

The practice has a range of "social classes" on their list, around 25% of the patients are recognised as being "deprived".

The statement of fees and allowances for quarters ending 30 June 1997, 30 September 1997, 31 December 1997 and 31 March 1998.

Seniority allowances are made to Drs A Brayne and C Drane at 2nd level and Dr D Payne at 1st level of payment.

The schedules of non-NHS income for the above quarters were also provided by the partnership.

The stock of drugs was valued at 31 March 1998 as £4,750.

Chapter 3

*Preparatory work
to the Financial Accounting*

The case study is not concerned with the bookkeeping and record keeping in detail, only with the accounts. The first few pages summarise the information that goes into the preparation of accounts for the financial year ended 31 March 1998.

1. The opening trial balance is a list of the balance on each of the accounts in the Nominal Ledger on the first day of the financial year, 1 April 1997, before any transactions have taken place.

2. The East Road Surgery maintains its bookkeeping on a computer programme and so each Nominal Ledger has a code as well as a description. A trial balance taken from a manual system would look exactly the same but without the code numbers down the left-hand side. A fuller explanation of the various accounts listed will be given as we go through the financial accounts later in this chapter.

3. Both sides of a trial balance are equal in value. If they are not, then an error has been made, which must be found and corrected before proceeding further.

Trial balance at

1 April 1997:

Code	Description	Debit	Credit
142	Stock of drugs	3750	
370	Freehold property	155000	
375	Improvement to property	28600	
380	Furniture, fixtures and fittings	21815	
382	Prov. for dep'n. Furn.fix.fit.		7833
385	Computer equipment	9750	
387	Prov. for dep'n Comp.Equip.		3832
390	Office & medical equip.	17550	
392	Prov. for dep'n Office & med.		7587
419	Hire purchase creditor		25255
421	HP Interest Suspense	3990	
450	Debtors - HA	22116	
455	Bank Deposit	8320	
457	Bank Current	4993	
464	Creditors - Drugs		1675
	Gas		320
	Electric		475
	Tel/Mobile		475
	Locum		1450
	Laundry		115
	Accountancy		2250
	PAYE/NIC		3963
469	Mortgage on property		136400
	Re-mortgage on property		28600
470	Property Capital: Dr A Brayne		9300
471	Dr C Drane		9300
480	Fixed Capital: Dr A Brayne		15000
	Dr C Drane		15000
490	Current Capital: Dr A Brayne		3527
	Dr C Drane		3527
		-----------	-----------
		£275884	£275884
		-----------	-----------

On the following pages are summarised the NHS income of the East Road Surgery Practice for the year ended 31 March 1998 by quarter. These are based on the 'Red Book' Statement of Fees and Allowances (see Exhibit 1 & 2).

As a further illustration some of the detailed workings are set out in note form below:-

Cervical Cytology (Note 1 in Exhibit 1)

Max. sum payable:

No. of eligible women
on partners' list   Lower target payment
-----------------------------   x   per quarter
430* x No. of partners

* No. of eligible women on the average GP list is 430 women.

Step 1: 80% target = 0.80 x (1800 - 25)
$$= 1420.00$$

50% target = 0.50 x (1800 - 25)
$$= 887.50$$

Step 2: Target reached 1440 - 12 already had smear test.
$$= 1428.00$$

Step 3: $\dfrac{1800 - 25 **}{430 \text{ x no. of partners}}$ x $\dfrac{2610}{4}$ =

**do not have a cervix.

$$\dfrac{1775}{1290} \quad x \quad 652.50 \ = \ 897.82$$

Step 4: GMS prop. = $\dfrac{1440}{1420}$ = > 100%

Step 5: Max. payment x GMS prop.

897.82 x 100%   = 897.82
Step 6: 897.82 x 3 partners   = 2,693.46 per quarter

STATEMENT OF FEES AND ALLOWANCES - Exhibit 1

Drs A Brayne, C Drane & D Payne		Rate £	Quarter to 30.6.97 No.	Amount	Quarter to 30.9.97 No.	Amount
Basic Practice Allowance				5616		5616
Seniority	#			1329		1329
Post Graduate Allowance				1770		1770
Registrar Scheme	#			1285		1285
Std. Capitation	<65	4.013	6025	24178	6055	24299
Std. Capitation	65-74	5.300	940	4982	1020	5406
Std. Capitation	>74	10.250	735	7534	815	8354
Deprivation Payment (Area 1)		2.800	694	1943	664	1859
Deprivation Payment (Area 2)		2.100	636	1336	645	1355
Deprivation Payment (Area 3)		1.613	673	1086	695	1121
Registration Fees		7.200	320	2304	120	864
Child Health Surveillance		2.913	433	1261	445	1296
Childhood Immunisation Aged 2	#			3191		3191
Pre School Boosters Aged 5	#			682		682
Cervical Cytology (Note 1)	#			**2693**		**2693**
Health Promotion				2283		2283
Asthma Management				296		296
Diabetes Management				296		296
Minor Surgery		1116.800	6	701	8	934
Vaccin. & Immunisation Type A		3.900	175	683	165	644
Vaccin. & Immunisation Type B		5.650	135	763	155	876
Contraceptive Services Fees		3.725	490	1825	479	1784
Intra Uterine Device Fee		12.000	56	672	72	864
Temp. Residence Up to 15 Days		9.450	32	302	33	312
Temp. Residence Over 15 Days		14.200	28	398	34	483
Immediate Necessary Treatment		9.450	12	113	23	217
Emergency Treatment		23.600	13	307	14	330
Night Visits		21.650	162	3507	167	3616
Out of Hours Quarterly Allow.				541		541
Maternity Medical Services		108.500	34	3689	25	2713
Total Gross				**77566**		**77308**

	Amount		Amount	
Less Deductions				
Advance Recoveries	44000		45000	
Recovery of Leave Payment	1125		1125	
		45125		46125
69.1% SR Items	47255		47076	
# 100% SR Items	9180		9180	
	56435		56256	
Superannuation Contribution		3386		3375
Dr A Brayne	1411		1406	
Dr C Drane	1129		1125	
Dr D Payne	846		844	
Net Amount Due		**£29055**		**£27808**
SR= Superannuable				

Childhood Immunisation (Note 2 in Exhibit 2)

Max. sum payable:

No. of children
(age group) on
Partnership list * *   Max. sum payable
------------------- x   to average GP.   x ***GMS prop. x No. of partners
22* x no. of partners   quarterly

* National average for one GP's list is 22 children.

Step 1: 130 children** x   4 groups   = 520 max. completing immunisation.

Step 2: Say 432 children immunised.   = 92% prop.
           Therefore, its 90% target reached.

Step 3: GMS prop.*** = $\dfrac{\text{No. of doses given by GPs}}{\text{90\% target x 520 child.}}$

$$\frac{130}{22 \times 3} \times £585 \times \frac{432}{468} \times 3 = £3,191 \text{ per quarter.}$$

Pre School Booster (Note 3 in Exhibit 2)

Step 1: 96 children** x   4 groups = 384 max. completing immunisation.

Step 2: Say 313 children immunised = 90.5% prop.
           Therefore, its 90% target reached.

Step 3: GMS prop.*** = $\dfrac{\text{No. of doses given by GPs}}{\text{90\% target x 384 child.}}$

$$\frac{96}{22 \times 3} \times £172.50 \times \frac{313}{346} \times 3 = £682 \text{ per quarter.}$$

STATEMENT OF FEES AND ALLOWANCES - Exhibit 2

Drs A Brayne, C Drane & D Payne	Rate £	Quarter to 31.12.97 No.	Amount	Quarter to 31.3.98 No.	Amount
Basic Practice Allowance			5616		5616
Seniority #			1329		1329
Post Graduate Allowance			1770		1770
Registrar Scheme #			1285		1285
Std. Capitation <65	4.013	6085	24419	5995	24058
Std. Capitation 65-74	5.300	1050	5565	1050	5565
Std. Capitation >74	10.250	845	8661	845	8661
Deprivation Payment (Area 1)	2.800	628	1758	643	1800
Deprivation Payment (Area 2)	2.100	680	1428	695	1460
Deprivation Payment (Area 3)	1.613	695	1121	662	1068
Registration Fees	7.200	30	216	120	864
Child Health Surveillance	2.913	457	1331	469	1366
Childhood Immun. Aged 2 (Note 2)	**#**		**3191**		**3191**
Pre School Boosters Aged 5 (Note 3)	**#**		**682**		**682**
Cervical Cytology	#		2693		2694
Health Promotion			2283		2284
Asthma Management			296		296
Diabetes Management			296		296
Minor Surgery	116.800	14	1635	15	1752
Vaccin. & Immunisation Type A	3.900	160	624	155	605
Vaccin. & Immunisation Type B	5.650	145	819	135	763
Contraceptive Services Fees	3.725	689	2567	708	2637
Intra Uterine Device Fee	12.000	87	1044	98	1176
Temp. Residence Up to 15 Days	9.450	44	416	35	331
Temp. Residence Over 15 Days	14.200	30	426	36	511
Immediate Necessary Treatment	9.450	12	113	16	151
Emergency Treatment	23.600	17	401	4	94
Night Visits	21.650	137	2966	142	3074
Out of Hours Quarterly Allow.			541		541
Maternity Medical Services	108.500	32	3472	27	2930
Total Gross			**78965**		**78850**

Less Deductions:		Amount		Amount	
Advance Recoveries		45000		50000	
Recovery of Leave Payment		1251		1125	
			46125		51125
69.1% SR Items		48221		48141	
# 100% SR Items		9180		9181	
		57401		57322	
Superannuation Contribution			3444		3439
Dr A Brayne		1435		1433	
Dr C Drane		1148		1147	
Dr D Payne		861		859	
Net Amount Due			**£29396**		**£24286**
SR = Superannuable					

Exhibits 3 & 4 show the reimbursements receivable from the HA on the basis of the 'Red Book'.

Notes:

(1)   Notional rent is based on a district valuer's assessment of the current market rent. The amount is reimbursed from the HA on a quarterly basis.

(2)   The business rates include water, sewerage, environment, and so on.

(3)   Under Practice Staff Scheme, 70% of the staff costs are reimbursed (refer to Exhibit 7).

(4)   Under GP Registrar Scheme, salary and costs are fully reimbursed (refer to Exhibit 7).

(5)   Under Computer Reimbursement Scheme, computer maintenance costs are reimbursed.

(6)   Practice Allowance relates to the employment of a full time assistant.

STATEMENT OF FEES AND ALLOWANCES - Exhibit 3

Dr A Brayne, C Drane & D Payne

		Qtr to 30.6.97		Qtr to 30.9.97	
(1) Notional rent			3506		3506
(2) Rates & Water			862		862
(3) Practice Staff Budget			17875		17875
(4) Registrar salary			6240		6240
Training Costs			1985		1985
(5) Computer Maintenance			800		800
	(Non SR)		31268		31268
(6) Employment of an Assistant	(SR)		1629		1629
(7) Prescribing Drugs Payments	(Non SR)				
Basic Prices (expenses)		3504		3743	
Discount (5%)		-175		-187	
Container All.		13		14	
VAT thereon 17.5%		585		625	
			3927		4195
Prescribing Drug Payments	(SR)				
On Cost (10.5% of Basic Price)		368		393	
Dispensing Fees (99.3% of no. of prescriptions)	325		347		
			693		740
Total			**37517**		**37832**
Non SR Items		35195		35463	
69.1% SR Items		2322		2369	
(8) 6% of:		1605		1637	
			96		99
Dr A Brayne		32		33	
Dr C Drane		32		33	
Dr D Payne		32		33	
Net Amount Due			**£37421**		**£37733**

(7)   The Practice receives the payment for the supply of drugs and appliances to patients. The Exhibit shows the quarterly payment allocated into two parts:

  (a)   Non SR part includes:
    The basic price less any discount as per the "Red Book".
    Container allowance for each prescription and any VAT incurred.

  (b)   SR part includes:
    An on cost allowance of 10.5% of the basic price before deducting any discount.
    A dispensing fee of 99.3% of the number of prescriptions.

(8)   GPs contribute to the NHS Pension Scheme and their income is allocated in to three groups:

  (a)   Non Superannuable Income
  (b)   100% Superannuable Income
  (c)   Partly Superannuable Income, in this case 69.1%

  6% of the Superannuable Income is contributed towards the NHS Pension Scheme. The SR deductions by the HA are allocated to the partners in their profit sharing ratios. At the end of the tax year, GPs receive an annual statement from the HA stating the amount deducted from their income.

STATEMENT OF FEES AND ALLOWANCES - Exhibit 4
Dr A Brayne, C Drane & D Payne

		Qtr to 31.12.97		Qtr to 31.3.98	
(1) Notional Rent			3506		3506
(2) Rates & Water			862		862
(3) Practice Staff Budget			17875		17875
(4) Registrar Salary			6240		6240
Training Costs			1985		1985
(5) Computer Maintenance			800		800
	(Non SR)		31268		31268
(6) Employment of an assistant	(SR)		1629		1629
(7) Prescribing Drugs Payments (Non SR)					
Basic Prices (expenses)		3927		3607	
Discount (5%)		-196		-180	
Container Allow		15		13	
VAT thereon 17.5%		655		602	
			4401		4042
Prescribing Drug Payments	(SR)				
On Cost (10.5% of Basic Price)		412		378	
Dispensing Fees		365		336	
(99.3% of no. of prescriptions)					
			777		714
Total			38075		37653
Non SR Items		35669		35310	
69.1% SR Items		2406		2343	
(8) 6% of:		1663		1619	
			99		96
Dr A Brayne		33		32	
Dr C Drane		33		32	
Dr D Payne		33		32	
Net Amount Due			**£37976**		**£37557**

Exhibit 5 and 6

Non NHS Work

There are no restrictions imposed upon the GPs on the amount of Non NHS work they do as long as they fulfil their NHS commitment. GPs can earn private income of less than 10% of total gross income. Should the private proportion exceed 10%, then an abatement rule applies. This means that NHS reimbursements will be reduced in accordance with a single scale. Income received from public sources is excluded. Also income from private work may be excluded from the computation of both the private earnings and the total practice income provided that the work is wholly performed away from the practice premises and no practice staff are involved.

(1) Income received from Nursing Home and University lectures are BMA Category D fees - fees as suggested by the BMA.

(2) Police Surgeon's fees are BMA Category B fees - fees negotiated nationally by the BMA with local government employers' organisations.

(3) Dr Brayne has a part-time hospital appointment. The fees are paid into the practice account in accordance with the partnership's policy. NT coding is obtained from the tax district dealing with the hospital appointment. It is assumed that the Tax Inspector has taken a practical view and has allowed such a code to operate. Income from such an appointment is paid without deduction of tax. Gross income forms part of the partnership income under Schedule D assessment.

(4) Patients examined, and reports provided to the insurance companies under BMA Category C fees.

(5) Cremation forms signed under BMA Category D fees.

(6) Private patients treated under BMA fee guidance.

NON NHS INCOME - Exhibit 5

Drs A Brayne, C Drane and D Payne.	SR Item	Quarter to 30.6.97	Quarter to 30.9.97
(1) Nursing Home		655	735
(1) University		325	175
(2) Police Surgeon's Fees		3150	2975
		4130	3885
(3) General Hospital Sch. E (NT Code)100%		3041	3041
Total		7171	6926
Superannuation Contributions:			
Dr A Brayne	6%	182	182
OTHER FEES			
(4) Insurance Examinations		505	475
(5) Cremations			65
(6) Private Patients		275	325
Total		**£780**	**£865**

NON NHS INCOME - Exhibit 6

Drs A Brayne, C Drane and D Payne.	SR Item	Quarter to 31.12.97	Quarter to 31.3.98
(1) Nursing Home		965	455
(1) University		225	445
(2) Police Surgeon's Fees		3050	2350
		4240	3250
(3) General Hospital Sch. E (NT Code)	100%	3041	3041
Total		7281	6291
Superannuation Contributions:			
Dr A Brayne	6%	182	182
OTHER FEES			
(4) Insurance Examinations		495	510
(5) Cremations			130
(6) Private Patients		475	525
Total		**£970**	**£1165**

The East Road Surgery - Exhibit 7

Payroll 1997/98	Code	Gross	Tax	NI E'yee	Net	NI E'yer
Dr E Zain	524H	36000	5583	2160	28258	2600
Mr S Patel: Bus.Manager	524H	24000	4191	2141	17669	2399
Ms E Brown: Prac.Manager	404L	16200	2673	1363	12164	1621
Ms J Yong: Prac.Nurse	404L	12000	1707	941	9353	1199
Ms A Black: Prac.Nurse	404L	8000	791	542	6667	400
Ms S Cooke: Rec/sec.	404L	6000	391	341	5268	299
Ms T Smith: Rec/Sec.	404L	6000	391	341	5268	299
Ms S Hall: Secretary	404L	6000	391	341	5268	299
Ms H Hope: Community Nurse	404L	8000	791	542	6667	400
Ms S Lane: Midwife	404L	8000	791	542	6667	400
Ms K White: Nurse	404L	625			625	
Total Ancillary staff:		94825	12116	7092	75617	7318
Part time staff		9600			9600	
Overall Total:		**140425**	**17699**	**9252**	**113475**	**9918**

Registrar Salary:

Dr M Lee	524H	24000	3859	2141	16560	2399
Less Superann. Contrib.6%		1440	Allowable for Tax but not for NIC.			
		22560				

		Cost:	Reimbursement
	Gross	94825	
	Ni'yer	7318	
		102143 x 70%	71500

Registrar Salary Inc NIC.	100%	26400
Less Superann. Contrib.		-1440
		£24960

The payroll programme produces reports such as periodical summaries, Inland Revenue Remittance Reports, Year End Reports and so on. This is all done "in house". The payroll figures reflect in Exhibit 8 which is a quarterly summary of the Nominal Ledger print out.

Note:

Reconciliation:	Exhibit 8		Exhibit 7	
Staff Salaries net	113475	Gross Salaries	140425	
PAYE & NIC	36868	Employers' NIC	9918	
	------------		------------	
	150343		150343	
	------------		------------	

The East Road Surgery - Exhibit 8

Surgery Expenses Qtr to:	30/6/97	30/9/97	31/12/97	1/3/98	TOTAL
Practice Expenses:					
Drugs	3705	3850	4145	6045	17745
Medical Instruments	2450	2015	2395	2225	9085
Medical Books, Journals, etc	725	865	685	785	3060
Courses and Conferences	1415	1335	1415	1855	6020
	£8295	£8065	£8640	£10910	£35910
Premises Costs:					
Rates and Water	862	862	862	862	3448
Light and Heat	1235	1325	1535	1465	5560
Insurance	656	656	656	656	2624
Use of Home	300	300	300	300	1200
	£3053	£3143	£3353	£3283	£12832
Employee Cost:					
Staff Salaries Net	28368	28368	28368	28371	**113475**
PAYE and NIC	9217	9217	9217	9217	**36868**
Registrar Salary	6240	6240	6240	6240	**24960**
Training Expenses	815	815	815	815	3260
Locum Fees	1825	2965	2775	3575	11140
Staff Welfare	1375	1180	1235	1063	4853
	£47840	£48785	£48650	£49281	£194556
Administration Expenses:					
Printing and Stationery	345	325	355	365	1390
Postage and Couriers	245	385	355	395	1380
Subscriptions	1090	1090	1090	1090	4360
Telephone and Mobile	1370	1710	1660	1800	6540
Cleaning and Laundry	575	585	575	585	2320
	£3625	£4095	£4035	£4235	£15990
Repair and Maintenance:					
Building Repairs	2725	3015	1335	3855	10930
Equipment Repairs	1655	1495	1780	1555	6485
Computer Maintenance	800	800	800	800	3200
	£5180	£5310	£3915	£6210	£20615
Motor & Travel Expenses:					
Car Running Expenses	2250	2250	2250	2250	9000
	£2250	£2250	£2250	£2250	£9000
Legal and Professional:					
Solicitors costs	195	265	275	350	1085
Accountancy fees	825	825	825	1575	4050
	£1020	£1090	£1100	£1925	£5135

Exhibit 9 and 10

This Exhibit shows Mortgage on freehold property and the additional borrowing being repaid over the years and final amounts outstanding. Annual repayments are allocated to the partners.

Interest on Mortgage

Interest on Mortgage statements received from the bank annually are summarised and listed over the years for record purposes. The quarterly summary of the nominal ledger print out reflects in Exhibit 10, which includes surgery loan interest.

Depreciation is provided on a reducing balance method and is summarised in Exhibit 10.

Hire Purchase Schedule is provided by the practice. The annual interest charged is correctly posted in the nominal ledger print out, i.e. the summary of expenses and agreed with the Schedule both of which are in Exhibit 10.

The East Road Surgery - Exhibit 9

Mortgage on Freehold Property

Date borrowed	Repay.	Initial borrowing £	Additional borrowing £	Dr A Brayne £	Dr C Drane £	Dr D Payne £
1.4.94		155000				
	31.3.95	-6200		-3100	-3100	
	31.3.96	-6200		-3100	-3100	
	31.3.97	-6200		-3100	-3100	
1.4.97			28600			
		136400	28600	-9300	-9300	
	31.3.98	-6200	-1300	-2500	-2500	-2500
		130200	27300	-11800	-11800	-2500

Interest on Mortgage

Year	Rate.	Balance B/fwd £	Payment £	Cumulative Principal £	Cumulative Interest £	Balance C/fwd £
1994/95	7.69%	155000	-13973	2131	11842	152869
31.3.95	Adjust		-4069	4069		-4069
		155000	-18042	6200	11842	148800
1995/96	7.97%	148800	-13925	2149	11776	146651
31.3.96	Adjust		-4051	4051		-4051
		148800	-17976	6200	11776	142600
1996/97	8.24%	142600	-13848	2174	11674	140426
31.3.97	Adjust		-4026	4026		-4026
		142600	-17874	6200	11674	136400
1997/98	8.56%	136400				
1.4.97	Addition	28600				
		165000	-16680	2655	**14025**	162345
31.3.98	Adjust		-4845	4845		-4845
		165000	-21525	7500	**14025**	157500

The East Road Surgery - Exhibit 10

Surgery Expenses	Qtr to:	30/6/97	30/9/97	31/12/97	31/3/98	TOTAL
	£	£	£	£	£	£
Interest:						
Bank Interest		565	683	485	332	2065
Surgery Loan Interest		3506	3506	3506	3507	**14025**
		4071	4189	3991	3839	16090
Other Finance Charges:						
Bank Charges		235	364	352	345	1296
H P Interest re Equip.		499	499	499	499	1996
H P Interest re Motor Vehicles		1800	1800	1800	1800	7200
Equipment Leasing		200	200	200	200	800
		2734	2863	2851	2844	11292
Depreciation:						
Furniture, Fixtures and Fittings		873	874	874	874	3495
Computer Equipment		369	370	370	370	1479
Medical and Office Equipment		622	623	623	623	2491
Motor Vehicles		3300	3300	3315	3315	13230
		5164	5167	5182	5182	20695

Motor Vehicles		Dr Brayne	Dr Drane	Dr Payne	Total
		£	£	£	£
Acquired on 6.4.97		17640	17640	17640	52920
H P Deposit paid		1440	1440	1440	4320
Finance by HP (36 Instal.)		16200	16200	16200	48600
H P Charges		4800	4800	4800	14400
Total cost		21000	21000	21000	63000
1st Year	Cost	5400	5400	5400	16200
	Int.	2400	2400	2400	7200
	Repay.	7800	7800	7800	23400
2nd Year	Cost	5400	5400	5400	16200
	Int.	1620	1620	1620	4860
	Repay.	7020	7020	7020	21060
3rd Year	Cost	5400	5400	5400	16200
	Int.	780	780	780	2340
	Repay.	6180	6180	6180	18540

Fixed Assets

Fixed Assets are those required for the practice to operate from day to day and so earn its income, but which have a working life measured in years. The working life of different assets may vary considerably. For example, a desk will normally have a very long life whereas a computer system, because of rapid advances in technology, may have a relatively short life of say 3-5 years. The costs of such assets is written off over the expected lifetime by using an appropriate method of depreciation (see next page).

East Road Surgery
Schedule of Fixed Assets
(excluding Freehold Property)

	Furniture Fixtures & Fittings £	Computer Equipment £	Office & Medical Equipment £	Total £
Year 1 (to 31.3.95)				
Cost of: Acquisitions	7,250	8,500	9,750	25,500
Less: NHS Grant	-	(4,250)	-	(4,250)
	7,250	4,250	9,750	21,250
Depreciation for Year	(1,813)	(1,063)	(2,438)	(5,314)
Net Book Value (NBV) at Year End	5,437	3,187	7,312	15,936
Year 2 (to 31.3.96)				
No Additions				
Depreciation for Year	(1,359)	(797)	(1,828)	(3,984)
NBV at Year End	4,078	2,390	5,484	11,952
Year 3 (31.3.97)				
Cost of:Additions	14,565	11,000	7,800	33,365
Less: NHS Grant	-	(5,500)	-	(5,500)
Depreciation for Year	(4,661)	(1,972)	(3,321)	(9,954)
NBV at Year End	13,982	5,918	9,963	29,863
Year 4 (to 31.3.98)				
No Additions				
Depreciation for Year	(3,495)	(1,479)	(2,491)	(7,465)
NBV at Year End	10,487	4,439	7,472	22,398
Summary to End of Year 4				
Cost (Net of Grants)	21,815	9,750	17,550	49,115
Accumulated Depreciation	11,328	5,311	10,078	26,717
NBV AT 31.3.98	10,487	4,439	7,472	22,398

Depreciation of Fixed Assets

There are several methods of depreciation, three of which are described below. The straight-line and the reducing-balance methods are the most commonly used in small businesses. The East Road Surgery has adopted a policy of depreciating its assets (other than freehold property) at a rate of 25% on the reducing balance.

Straight Line Method

An equal amount of cost is written off each year. For example, an asset is purchased for £1,000 with an expected useful life of 10 years and an estimated residual value of £50. The £950 of depreciation would be written off at £95 each year. This method is suitable for those assets whose useful value to the practice is fairly even over the assets' lifetime, such as furniture.

Reducing Balance Method

The asset is depreciated unevenly over its lifetime by using a fixed rate and applying it to the cost (in the first year) and then the book value (in subsequent years). For example, as asset costing £1,200 is written off by 25% per annum by this method. The first year write-off is £300 (25% x £1,200); in the second year £225 (25% x £900); and so on. The useful working life should be estimated and the rate of depreciation to use is double what the rate would have been under the straight line method.

This method is suitable where the value deteriorates more rapidly in the early years and where maintenance costs increase with its age, such as motor vehicles.

Sum-of-the-Years' Digits

This method is similar to the reducing balance method. An asset costing £1,500 has an expected useful life of five years after which its value would be negligible. Add the years together (5+4+3+2+1 = 15); then depreciate by 5/15 x £1,500 in year one (£500); then 4/15 in year two (£450) and so on.

Net Book Value of Fixed Assets

Fixed Assets enable the practice to be carried on. They are not bought and sold for profit. The book value of assets (i.e. the original cost less the amount so far written off by way of depreciation) should therefore be seen in the context of the practice's depreciation policy and must not be confused with second-hand value or replacement cost, both of which may be quite different.

The book value is dependent upon the practice being a 'going concern'. As long as the practice continues to operate then the assets are worth their book value. If, however, the practice ceased, then the second-hand sale value may be materially different, usually (except for premises) considerably lower. For example, waiting room chairs which, are several years old may have virtually no second-hand value but have an obvious value to the practice. Patients would not find it acceptable to stand, and it would be exorbitantly expensive to replace the chairs on an annual basis.

It is difficult in practice to accurately forecast the useful working life of assets and to estimate their residual value. The Fixed Assets register should be examined on a regular basis. Assets which have reached the end of their 'real' useful life, through wear and tear or obsolescence, should be scrapped and written out the books by writing off the net book value, less the amount of any proceeds from sale, as additional depreciation in that year. On the other hand, some assets may have been almost depreciated to zero but still in fact have some continuing use to the practice. These should be kept on the books at a nominal value, say £1 so that no further depreciation is charged for them but their existence is still recorded in the books. If an asset is sold for a price, which exceeds its book value then the difference is often shown in accounts as 'Profit on Disposal of Fixed Assets. The 'profit' merely indicates that the sale proceeds have exceeded the written-down value. For example, a motor car costing £8,000 has been written down to £2,500 but is in fact sold for cash (or part-exchange value) for £3,000. The £500 would appear in the accounts as a 'Profit on Disposal.....,' It is effectively a writing-back of depreciation.

Having started with the opening trial balance as shown at the beginning of this chapter, and having posted to the Nominal Ledger accounts all the income and expenditure transactions shown in the summary on the preceding pages, a further trial balance is extracted from the Nominal Ledger on the final day of the financial year.

From this trial balance the financial accounts of the practice for the year will be prepared using the accounting principles, as explained later.

Trial Balance at 31 March 1998

Code	Description	Debit £	Credit £
7	Practice Allowances		46515
8	Capitation Fees		178517
9	Target Payments		26265
10	Chronic Dis. & Health Prom.		11501
11	Sessional Payments		5022
12	Item of Service		51385
14	Other NHS Fees		2924
15	Reimbursements		141639
16	Appointments		27669
17	Non NHS Fees		3780
142	Stock of Drugs	3750	
145	Stock of Drugs		4750
201	Bank Interest Receivable		1500
210	Practice Expenses	35910	
228	Premises Costs	12832	
237	Repairs and Renewals	20615	
244	Administration Expenses	15990	
251	Employee Costs	194556	
268	Motor and Travel	9000	
275	Legal & Professional	5135	
314	Other Finance Charges	11292	
315	Interest	16090	
332	Depreciation	20695	
370	Freehold Property	180250	
375	Improvement to Property	28600	
380	Furniture Fixtures & Fittings	21815	
382	Prov. for Dep'n Furn F & F		11328
385	Computer Equipment	9750	
387	Prov.for Dep'n Computers		5311
390	Office & Medical Equip.	17550	
392	Prov. for Dep'n Med.Equip		10078
402	Motor Vehicles	52920	
407	Depreciation - Vehicles		13230
419	Hire Purchase Account 1		12628
421	H P Interest Suspense 1	1994	
423	Hire Purchase Account 2		39600
425	H P Interest Suspense 2	7200	
447	Stock of Drugs	4750	
450	Debtors and Prepayments	61843	
455	Bank Deposit Account	2477	
457	Bank Current Account		9261
460	Cash in Hand	50	
464	Creditors / Accrued Charges		19567
469	Mortgage Account		157500

ctd...........

........ctd

Trial Balance at 31 March 1998 (ctd)

Code	Description	Debit £	Credit £
470	Prop.Capital Dr A Brayne		8700
471	Prop.Capital Dr C Drane		8700
472	Prop.Capital Dr D Payne		8700
480	Fixed Capital Dr A Brayne		23000
481	Fixed Capital Dr C Drane		23000
482	Fixed Capital Dr D Payne		23000
490	Current Acc.Dr A Brayne	48291	
491	Current Acc.Dr C Drane	46427	
492	Current Acc.Dr D Payne	45288	
	PROFIT AND LOSS ACCOUNT TOTALS	345865	501467
	BALANCE SHEET TOTALS	529205	373603
		1750140	1750140
155602	**NET PROFIT**		

The above Trial Balance is extracted after posting all the transactions of the East Road Surgery for the year ended 31 March 1998.

Chapter 4

Financial Accounting

Financial Accounting

Financial accounting is concerned with the collection of information regarding financial transactions, expressed in monetary terms, and day to day recording of that information in books of account. At the end of the accounting period, this financial information is summarised and presented in the form of a Profit and Loss account and Balance Sheet. This is historical information and is reported in accordance with the provision of the Statement of Fees and Allowances and generally accepted accounting principles. These financial statements are then used by third parties such as the Inland Revenue and banks.

Collection of information and daily recording of transactions

Some of the prime documents from which the books are written up are listed as follows:

(a)   Periodical statements of fees and allowances received from HA. This provides analytical information on income received.
(b)   Invoices from suppliers to evidence the cost, date and description of purchases.
(c)   Chequebook stubs to record details of cheques issued and paying in books to record cheques/cash received.
(d)   Bank statements to check clearance of cheques, direct debits, standing orders and to record bank charges.
(e)   Petty cash vouchers to record cash expenses.
(f)   Wages sheets to record employee cost.

Summarised financial information

At the end of the accounting period, when all the documents have been recorded in the books of account, a trial balance is extracted showing a summary of total balances recorded in ledger accounts - a valuable check on the accuracy of the bookkeeping. This means when every transaction is entered as a debit with a corresponding entry as a credit, total debit balances equal total credit balances. Once the trial balance is prepared, it can be used as a basis for preparing a Profit and Loss account and Balance Sheet.

Historical information

Financial accounting is concerned with reporting historical information. This means that the historical cost of an asset is the monetary cost of its acquisition. However, subjective opinions are important in historical cost accounting.

Examples:

Stock may be stated at net realisable value where this is estimated to be less than the cost.

Depreciation charges require subjective estimates of useful life and estimated scrap value at the end of the useful life.

A freehold property may be stated at a re-valued figure (this may be different from the current value at the balance sheet date if the revaluation occurred some time ago).

Compliance with the NHS General Medical Services SFAs (Red Book)

The Red Book has detailed guidance on the treatment of different items of income and expenditure in the accounts. It advises that the 'grossing up' principle should be applied where the HA meets a revenue expense directly, or indirectly. When presenting the practice accounts, the maximum amount is shown for expenses rather than netting off expenses against reimbursements.

Compliance with generally accepted accounting principles

Accounting principles have developed gradually over the years as the best way to solve problems that arise in accounting. These are rules that govern existing practice of account preparation. They represent a generally agreed way of presenting the financial statements. These are:

(a)　Continuity of existence: In the absence of information to the contrary, it is presumed that the firm will carry on medical practice for an indefinite period. It will continue to provide services to its patients in an orderly manner and derive the use from those assets not purchased for resale. Medical equipment held to provide services to patients would be valued for its use rather than at what price it will sell in the market. Where a firm is to cease business, a different approach to valuation and reporting is used.

(b)　Matching principles (accrual concept): It refers to matching of costs and revenues. Revenues are recognised as they are earned. Costs are recognised as they are incurred. The realisation of revenue means the date of service rather than the date when the cash relating to the service is received. Profit for the period should represent the earnings of the time, taking into account accrued expenses. Any costs concerning a future period must be carried forward as a prepayment.

(c)　Consistency: There is consistency of accounting treatment of similar items,
-　within each accounting period and
-　from one period to the next
Example: One medical practice may use the straight-line method, another practice may use the sum of the years' digits method. Each practice should be consistent in selecting the method for all assets in that class and for all accounting periods. Only in this way can a useful comparison of reported results over time be made.

(d)　Prudence: Revenue and profits should not be anticipated but all possible losses should be provided. This means that understatement of profits is preferable to overstatement of profits. The fear is that an optimistic approach may overstate profits and this may lead to distribution of income out of capital. A medical practice values its assets at the lowest possible values and liabilities at their highest possible values. Example: The valuation of stock at the lower of cost or net realisable value.

The figures on the opposite page are taken from the detailed accounts, which follow. These summaries illustrate the main points of the two principal financial accounting statements - the Profit and Loss Account and the Balance Sheet.

1. The Profit and Loss Account shows by way of financial measurement the activity of the practice over a period of time. The main Profit and Loss Account will cover a period of twelve months to the normal annual accounting date of the practice. The partners may also draw up a Profit and Loss Account for shorter periods (monthly, quarterly) to monitor progress through the financial year.

2. Income earned by the activities of the practice during the period from 1 April 1997 to 31 March 1998, whether received during that period or not (see Accruals Basis).

3. The expenses incurred during the same period, in earning the income in (2) whether or not the expenses were paid for in this period (see Accruals Basis).

4. The profit generated by the operating activities of the practice during the period, being the simple difference between Income (2) and Expenses (3).

5. Income earned on the practice bank deposit account is shown separately as this income derives from a non-active source and is not in itself generated by the activities of the partners and staff.

6. Similarly interest payable is an expense incurred because of the manner in which the practice is financed and not in itself incurred by the activities of the partners and staff.

7. The Net Profit is the net result of all income earned for the period after deducting all expenses for the period. If expenditure exceeded income then the result would have been a Net Loss.

8   The Net Profit (7) is then allocated between the partners in accordance with the Partnership Agreement. In this Case Study the allocation is a straightforward equal share of profit. The slightly lower figure for Dr Payne reflects that he was a partner for rather less than the full twelve-month period.

The account is sometimes shown as an Income and Expenditure Account. The authors are of the commonly accepted opinion that Income and Expenditure Account is an appropriate title for non-profit making organisations. Self-employed persons, whether professionals or not, earn their living by way of profit and we consider the title Profit and Loss Account to be the most appropriate for this account.

Appropriation of Profit may involve more than just simple profit shares. One or more partners may be entitled to a salary (with or without a further share of profit). If partners Capital Accounts are not equal then interest on Capital may be credited to allow for the imbalance. Appropriation of Profit would normally be made in the following order:-

1.   Salaries
2.   Interest on Capital
3.   The balance shared according to the partners' profit sharing ratios.

THE EAST ROAD SURGERY

Notes			
	Drs A Brayne, C Drane and D Payne		
	SUMMARY PROFIT AND LOSS ACCOUNT		
(1)	**FOR THE YEAR ENDED 31 MARCH 1998**		

		1998	**1997**
(2)	INCOME	495217	358321
(3)	LESS: EXPENSES	315829	245823
(4)	OPERATING PROFIT	179388	112498
(5)	ADD: INTEREST RECEIVABLE	1500	1250
(6)	LESS: INTEREST PAYABLE	(25286)	(12110)
(7)	NET PROFIT FOR THE YEAR	£155602	£101638
(8)	APPROPRIATION OF PROFIT		
	Dr A Brayne	52366	50819
	Dr C Drane	52366	50819
	Dr D Payne	50870	-
		£155602	£101638

9. A Balance Sheet is a summary of Assets, Liabilities and Capital as at a particular date. It is usual practice for a Balance Sheet to be drawn up to show the position at the close of business on the final day of the practice's annual accounting period. A Balance Sheet may be drawn up at any time to show the financial position of the practice and each partner's share in the Net Assets.

10. Assets with individual life expectancies exceeding one year are termed FixedAssets. They include items of Furniture, Medical Equipment, Computers, Freehold and Leasehold Property and Motor Vehicles. The original cost is then written off (Depreciated) over the life expectancy and so the cost is spread over several Profit and Loss Account periods. Some assets, such as Freehold Property, may actually increase in value over time and may be Re-valued for Balance Sheet purposes if current value is materially different from original cost and likely to remain so. As we shall see later in this Case Study, property was re-valued on the admission of a new partner.

11. Current Assets (e.g. Stock, Debtors, Cash at Bank, Cash in Hand). These are sometimes called circulating assets which, together with Current Liabilities (12) involve items that are changed into cash and back again. Stock is sold (to the NHS); the NHS become a Debtor for these goods and for services provided; the NHS pay their debt and the money is paid into the Bank Account; the money in the Bank Account is used to pay suppliers to the practice of goods and services.

12. Current Liabilities include Creditors for goods and services; the Inland Revenue for tax and insurance deducted from employees; the bank overdraft. Any debt that is due for payment during the following twelve months is deemed to be ' current' and would include instalments due under Hire Purchase Agreements and loan repayments. See also under Current Assets (11) above.

13. The net figure between Current Assets (11) and Current Liabilities (12) is usually referred to as the 'Working Capital' of the practice.

14. Long Term Liabilities are those where the repayments are beyond the next twelve month period. In this case they are Hire Purchase Contracts and Mortgage repayments. Instalments due within the next 12 months should be classed as current and included with Current Liabilities (12).

15. The Net Assets of the business represent the Capital invested by the partners. This may be Capital Introduced into the practice or the accumulation of profits left in the practice over one or more years. A simple way of viewing this item is this. If all the assets at the Balance Sheet date were disposed of at book value and all the liabilities paid off at book value, the partners would be left with £110,696 in cash to be split between them according to their individual capital accounts. It should be remembered that book values are based on the 'going concern' principle and assets may realise more or less than this figure if actually sold.

The Working Capital is the circulatory system of the practice. As well as being profitable, the practice must maintain a practice cash flow in order to survive. A 'rule of thumb' ratio between Current Assets and Current Liabilities to make life 'comfortable' is 2:1. The ratio will vary between different types of business and will also depend on the actual assets and liabilities involved. Because the NHS is a regular payer and without risk of becoming a bad debt, general practices can usually manage with a lower ratio.

Businesses with a very low or even negative Working Capital often experience difficulty in paying their bills on time.

THE EAST ROAD SURGERY

DRS A Brayne, C Drayne and D Payne
SUMMARY BALANCE SHEET

(9)   AS AT 31 MARCH 1998

		1998		1997
(10)	FIXED ASSETS		270938		213463
(11)	CURRENT ASSETS	69120		39179	
(12)	DEDUCT:				
	CURRENT LIABILITIES	(63162)		(39488)	
		----------		----------	
(13)	NET CURRENT ASSETS (LIABILITIES)		5958		(309)
			----------		----------
			276896		213154
(14)	DEDUCT:				
	LONG TERM LIABILITIES		166200		157500
			----------		----------
(15)	NET ASSETS		£110696		£55654
			=======		======
	PARTNERS' SHARE		£110696		£55654
			=======		======

Chapter 5

Presentation of the
Financial Statements

Drs A Brayne, C Drane and D Payne

THE EAST ROAD SURGERY

REPORT OF THE PARTNERS

The partners have pleasure in presenting their Annual Report and Accounts for the year ended 31 March 1998.

Practice Review

The partners consider that the state of affairs of the practice at the date of the Balance Sheet was satisfactory.

Results

The profit before tax for the year amounted to £155602 as shown on page 5.

Fixed Assets

Full details of the movements on the Fixed Assets Account are set out in the note 23 to these Accounts.

Future Developments

The practice will continue to develop along the lines successfully pursued in the current year.

Partners

The partners in the practice were:

> A Brayne
>
> C Drane
>
> D Payne, was introduced on 6 April 1997.

Their interest in the practice reflects in the Capital Accounts as shown in the note 25 to these Accounts.

By order of the Partnership

Dr A Brayne.

1

(1) Current Assets are listed in order of liquidity with the least liquid item, in this case Stock, being shown first and the most liquid item, Cash in Hand, being last.

(2) Prepayments are items of expense which are paid in advance and straddle more than one accounting period. Debtors are amounts receivable by the practice for services provided. In this instance all the debtors at 31.3.1998 were amounts due from the NHS.

(3) Current Liabilities are also shown in order of liquidity. Thus repayments due on HP and mortgage which are for the ensuing twelve months are shown first and the Bank Overdraft, which fluctuates daily and is repayable on demand, is shown last.

(4) The value of Net Current Assets (Working Capital) has improved to a position of £5958 compared to the position one year earlier when there was a deficit of working capital of £309.

(5) The mortgage is shown in detail in chapter 3.

(6) Net Asset value per partner has increased from £27,827 in 1997 (2 partners) to £36,898 in 1998 (3 partners).

Liquid assets are those which are held in cash or are readily convertible to cash. In the case study we would eliminate stock and prepayments. The Debtors figure is the amount due from the NHS and will be received at the end of the month. The liquid assets would therefore be £64370 (Debtors £61843 plus Bank/Cash £2527).

Liquidity is the ratio of liquid assets to the amount of Current Liabilities payable now or within a very short time. In the case study we can eliminate the mortgage and HP instalments due further away than one month. Similarly, the accruals. The remaining Current Liabilities are due now or at the end of the month (bank overdrafts are repayable on demand).

Drs A Brayne, C Drane and D Payne

THE EAST ROAD SURGERY

BALANCE SHEET
As at 31 March 1998

		Note	1998 £	£	1997 £	£
	FIXED ASSETS	23		270938		213463
(1)	CURRENT ASSETS:					
	Stock	1.5	4750		3750	
(2)	Debtors & Prepayments		61843		22116	
	Bank Deposit		2477		8320	
	Bank Current				4993	
	Cash in Hand		50			
			----------		----------	
			69120		39179	
			----------		----------	
(3)	CURRENT LIABILITIES:					
	Mortgage due		7500		7500	
	Hire Purchase Creditor	1.3	26834		21265	
	Creditors & Accruals		19567		10723	
	Bank Overdraft		9261			
			----------		----------	
			63162		39488	
			----------		----------	
(4)	NET CURRENT ASSETS(LIABILITIES)			5958		(309)
				----------		----------
				276896		213154
	LONG TERM LIABILITIES:					
(5)	Mortgage on Property		150000		157500	
	Hire Purchase Creditor		16200		-	
			----------		----------	
				166200		157500
				----------		----------
(6)	NET ASSETS			110696		55654
				----------		----------

2

49

(7) With the increase in partners from 2 to 3 and the increase in activity carried out by the practice (see Profit and Loss Account), the amount of capital that the partners have invested in the practice has virtually doubled from £55,654 to £110,696.

Property Capital Account

This account reflects the amount of each partner's interest in the equity of the partnership premises. Equity is the difference between the cost or valuation of the premises and the amount of any outstanding mortgage. Property Capital is a permanent investment and will normally increase in value as the mortgage is paid off out of annual profits.

Capital Account

This account reflects the amount of each partner's interest in the value of fixed assets (other than premises) and working capital.

Current Account

This account shows the balance of each partner's share of profits after deducting the amounts of drawings and transfers to capital accounts.

(8) The annual accounts should be formally discussed at a Partners' Meeting with the firm's accountant present and possibly the Business/Practice Managers. Once the accounts have been accepted by all Partners, they should be signed to that effect and become binding on all partners. They will form the basis of their Tax Returns (see Taxation chapter) and may be referred to in the event of a dissolution of the partnership or the admission of further partners. The accounts would also be material evidence for the continuing support of the bank borrowings and part of the basis for any future borrowings.

Drs A Brayne, C Drane and D Payne

THE EAST ROAD SURGERY

BALANCE SHEET
As at 31 March 1998

		Notes	1998	1997
			£	£
	FINANCED BY:			
(7)	PARTNERS' CAPITAL ACCOUNTS:			
	Dr A Brayne	25	35277	27827
	Dr C Drane	25	37140	27827
	Dr D Payne	25	38279	-
			110696	55654

(8)   ACCOUNTS APPROVAL CERTIFICATE

We approve the above Accounts and confirm that the accounting records produced, together with information and explanations supplied to Able Smart & Associates constitute a true and correct record of all the transactions of this practice for the year ended 31 March 1998.

....
Dr A Brayne

....
Dr C Drane

....
Dr D Payne   30 April 1998

3

Explanation of the Accountants' Report

The partners of The East Road Surgery should understand that their accountants are only confirming that they were instructed to prepare the financial statements but not to audit them. Therefore, the accountants' report should not be described as an audit report. However, there are times when the partners may require their books and records of the partnership to be audited. In such cases, the partners should instruct their independent accountants to carry out an audit. On this occasion the accountants will act as auditors and will report to the partners on the truth and fairness of the state of affairs of the partnership. The report will be described as an 'audit report'.

Drs A Brayne, C Drane and D Payne

THE EAST ROAD SURGERY

ACCOUNTANTS' REPORT

We have prepared, without undertaking an audit, the Accounts for the year ended 31 March 1998, set out on pages 2 to 14 from the books and records of the practice and from information and explanations supplied to us.

Able, Smart & Associates
Chartered Certified Accountants
Leicester   30 April 1998

4

This is the main Profit and Loss Account for the partnership's 'East Road Surgery' for the financial year ended 31 March 1998, together with the comparative figures for the preceding financial year.

(1) It is important for as much relevant information as possible to be disclosed in the financial statement, so that the partners can get a good financial 'picture' of the year under review. The Profit and Loss Account would be very cumbersome if all this information was detailed within it. Thus the information is presented under suitable headings and the detail is analysed in accompanying notes.

(2) Income is clearly shown under the main sources.

(3) Expenditure is also shown with a total for each main category and the analysis contained within the notes. This gives a clear view of the relative impact of each category in relation to the overall activity. For example, Staff Costs are 61.6% of total expenditure, whereas Travel and Subsistence accounts for just 0.7%. In the preceding year, Staff Costs were 65% of all expenditure. If items of expenditure and reimbursements had been 'netted-off' the figures would have looked very different.

(4) The Total Net Income represents the partners' earnings for the year and is the basis of their taxable income (see Taxation chapter, post).

Part of the evidence which the review Body considers when reviewing the 'Statement of Fees and Allowances' for the Cost-plus Contracts is a selection of accounts of General Practitioners provided at random by the Inland Revenue. Accounts which have been prepared on a 'netting-off' basis distort the real costs involved, and have been criticised as being part of the reason why target incomes have failed to be met.

Drs A Brayne, C Drane and D Payne

THE EAST ROAD SURGERY

PROFIT AND LOSS ACCOUNT
For the Year Ended 31 March 1998

		Notes	1998 £	1997 £
(1)				
(2)	INCOME:			
	Practice Allowances	2	48680	36813
	Capitation Fees	3	178517	131746
	Target Payments	4	26265	21102
	Chronic Disease Management and Health Promotion	5	11501	8721
	Sessional Payments	6	5022	3074
	Item of Service	7	49220	38067
	Gross National Health Service Income		319205	239523
	Other NHS Payments	8	2924	1948
	Reimbursements	9	141639	106760
	Appointments	10	27669	7573
	Other Fees	11	3780	2517
	TOTAL INCOME		495217	358321
(3)	EXPENDITURE:			
	Practice Expenses	12	34910	26264
	Premises Costs	13	12832	10959
	Employee Costs	14	194556	159325
	Administration Expenses	15	15990	11450
	Repairs & Renewals	16	20615	15724
	Motor Expenses	17	6750	4703
	Travel & Subsistence	18	2250	1694
	Legal & Professional	19	5135	3415
	Other Finance Charges	21	2096	2335
	Depreciation	23	20695	9954
	TOTAL EXPENDITURE		315829	245823
	OPERATING PROFIT FOR THE YEAR		179388	112498
(4)	INCOME FROM INVESTMENT	22	1500	1250
	Interest Payable	20	(25286)	(12110)
	TOTAL NET INCOME FOR THE YEAR		155602	101638

5

The Cash Flow statement shows where cash comes from and goes to during a particular time period.

The information for the cash flow statement is derived from both the Profit and Loss Account and the Balance Sheet.

Cash comes from both external and internal sources and flows from three main areas -operating activity, investment activity and financing activity.

It is important to read and understand the Financial Statements as a whole. The three principal reports each have a different purpose but are inextricably linked. The Profit and Loss Account shows in financial terms the activity of the practice over a given period; the relative activity of different areas of the practice; how the actual results turned out and compared to what the pre-determined plan was and this helps to plan financial activities. It shows each partners' income by way of their share of profits.

The Balance Sheet shows the net worth of the practice at a particular date; the relationship between assets and liabilities; the financial state of the practice at that particular date; each partner's share in the net worth of the practice.

The cash flow shows where the practice cash revenues have come from and how they were used; the movement, up or down, in the cash resources of the practice between two particular dates; the liquid revenue of the practice, its ability to pay its bills on time, and its continuing viability.

Drs A Brayne, C Drane and D Payne

THE EAST ROAD SURGERY

SOURCE AND DISPOSITION OF FUNDS
31 March 1998

	1998		1997	
	£	£	£	£
Source of Funds:				
Net Income	155602		101638	
Add back: Depreciation Provision	20695		9954	
Increase in Creditors	8844		6525	
Cash Introduced	30000		-	
	215141		118117	
Disposition of Funds:				
Deposit on Motor Vehicles	4320		-	
Hire Purchase Creditors repaid	26831		-	
Mortgage repaid	7500		6200	
Increase in Stock	1000		500	
Increase in Debtors	39727		35250	
Partners' Drawings	155810		101600	
	235188		143550	
Net Cash Outflow		(20047)		(25433)
Balance at 1 April 1997:				
Bank Current Account	4993			
Bank Deposit Account	8320			
		13313		38746
Balance at 31 March 1998:				
Cash account	50		-	
Bank Current account (Overdrawn)	(9261)		4993	
Bank Deposit account	2477		8320	
		(6734)		13313
Reduction in bank balances		(20,047)		(25433)

6

Drs A Brayne, C Drane and D Payne

NOTES TO THE ACCOUNTS
Year Ended 31 March 1998

Accounting Policies:

1.1 Basis of Accounting

The Accounts have been prepared:
(a) under the historical cost convention and reflect actual income earned, and expenditure incurred, during the year

(b) taking into account principles outlined in the General Medical Services' Statement of Fees and Allowances for General Medical Practitioners in England and Wales.

1.2 Depreciation

Depreciation is calculated to write off the cost of tangible fixed assets over their estimated useful lives to the practice. The annual depreciation rates and methods are as follows:

Furniture, fixtures and fittings	25% of net book value
Computer equipment	25% of net book value
Office and medical equipment	25% of net book value

The surgery freehold property is not depreciated.

1.3 Assets held under hire purchase contracts

Fixed assets held under hire purchase contracts, are treated as if purchased outright. The corresponding obligations are included in creditors.

Depreciation is provided by the rates and method set out above.

The related finance costs are charged to the Profit and Loss Account in proportion over the period of the contracts.

1.4 Operating Leases

Rentals under operating leases are charged on a straight-line basis over the lease term.

1.5 Stock

The stock of drugs is valued at the lower of cost or net realisable value.

Drs A Brayne, C Drane and D Payne
THE EAST ROAD SURGERY

NOTES TO THE ACCOUNTS

Year Ended 31 March

		1998	1997
		£	£
2.	Practice Allowances:		
	Basic Allowances	22464	14400
	Seniority allowances	5316	4650
	P G E allowances	7080	4520
	Assistance allowance	6515	6240
	Out of Hours allowance	2165	2078
	Registrar Scheme	5140	4925
		48680	36813
3.	Capitation fees:		
	Standard fees	151683	110228
	Deprivation fees	17331	12137
	Registration fees	4248	5146
	Child health surveillance fees	5255	4235
		178517	131746
4.	Target Payments:		
	Childhood Immunisation	12764	10294
	Pre School Boosters	2728	2209
	Cervical Cytology	10773	8599
		26265	21102
5.	Chronic Disease & Health Promotion:		
	Chronic disease management	9133	7091
	Health promotion clinic	2368	1630
		11501	8721
6.	Sessional Payments:		
	Minor Surgeries	5022	3074

7

Drs A Brayne, C Drane and D Payne

THE EAST ROAD SURGERY

NOTES TO THE ACCOUNTS

Year Ended 31 March 1998

		1998 £	1997 £
7.	Item of service:		
	Vaccinations & Immunisations	5776	4560
	Contraceptives	8814	7036
	Intra Uterine Devices	3756	3053
	Temporary residence	3179	2476
	Emergency treatment	1133	586
	Immediate treatment	596	485
	Night Visits	13163	10229
	Maternity	12804	9642
		49221	38067
8.	Other NHS Payments:		
	Dispensing	2924	1948
9.	Reimbursements:		
	Premises- Notional rent	14025	10695
	Rates and Water	3449	2630
	Staff - Salaries and NIC	71500	48500
	Trainee Salary	24960	23275
	Trainee Expenses	7940	7425
	Computer	3200	3200
	Drugs	16565	11035
		141639	106760
10.	Appointments:		
	General Hospital	12164	2225
	University	1170	-
	Police surgeon's fees	11525	2676
	Nursing Home	2810	2672
		27669	7573

8

Drs A Brayne, C Drane and D Payne

THE EAST ROAD SURGERY

NOTES TO THE ACCOUNTS

Year Ended 31 March 1998

		1998 £	1997 £
11.	Other Fees:		
	Insurance examinations	1985	1322
	Cremations	195	129
	Private Patients	1600	1066
		3780	2517
12.	Practice Expenses:		
	Drugs	16745	13158
	Medical Instruments	9085	7054
	Medical books, Journals and periodicals	3060	2039
	Courses and conferences	6020	4013
		34910	26264
13.	Premises Costs:		
	Rates and Water	3448	3299
	Light and heat	5560	4710
	Insurance	2624	2150
	Use of Home	1200	800
		12832	10959
14.	Employee Costs:		
	Staff Salaries	150341	111725
	Trainee Salary	24960	23275
	Trainee Expenses	3260	3170
	Staff Welfare	4855	3735
	Locum fees	11140	17420
		194556	159325

9

Drs A Brayne, C Drane and D Payne

THE EAST ROAD SURGERY

NOTES TO THE ACCOUNTS

Year Ended 31 March 1998

		1998 £	1997 £
15.	Administration Expenses:		
	Printing and Stationary	1390	1724
	Postage and Couriers	1380	1515
	Subscriptions	760	670
	Telephone and Mobile	6240	5496
	Cleaning and Laundry	2320	2045
		----------	----------
		12090	11450
		----------	----------
16.	Repairs and Maintenance:		
	Building Maintenance	10930	8207
	Equipment Repair	6485	4317
	Computer Maintenance	3200	3200
		----------	----------
		20615	15724
		----------	----------
17.	Motor Expenses:		
	Petrol	2715	1821
	Service & Repairs	2250	1667
	Car Insurance	1350	935
	Car Tax	435	280
		----------	----------
		6750	4703
		----------	----------
18.	Travel & Subsistence	2250	1694
		----------	----------
19.	Legal & Professional		
	Solicitors Costs	1085	720
	Accountancy fees	4050	2695
		----------	----------
		5135	3415
		----------	----------

10

Drs A Brayne, C Drane and D Payne

THE EAST ROAD SURGERY

NOTES TO THE ACCOUNTS

Year Ended 31 March 1998

		1998 £	1997 £
20.	Interest:		
	Bank Interest	2065	1415
	Surgery loan interest	14025	10695
	HP Interest re Equipment	1996	-
	HP Interest re Cars	7200	-
		25286	12110
21.	Other finance charges:		
	Bank Charges	1296	1535
	Equipment Leasing	800	800
		2096	2335
22.	Income from Investment:		
	Bank Deposit account Interest	1500	1250

11

Drs A Brayne, C Drane and D Payne
THE EAST ROAD SURGERY

NOTES TO THE ACCOUNTS

Year Ended 31 March 1998

23.   Fixed Assets:

	Surgery Freehold Property £	Improvements to property £	Total £
Cost:			
At 1 April 1997	155000	28600	183600
Revaluation Reserve			25250
At 31 March 1998			208850

	Furniture Fixtures & Fittings £	Computer Equipment £	Office & Medical Equipment £	Motor Vehicles £	Total £
Cost:					
At 1.4.1997	21815	9750	17550		49115
Additions				52920	52920
At 31.3.1998	21815	9750	17550	52920	102035
Depreciation:					
At 31.4.1997	7833	3832	7587		19252
Charge for year	3495	1479	2491	13230	20695
At 31.3.1998	11328	5311	10078	13230	39947
Net Book Value:					
At 31.3.1998	10487	4439	7472	39690	62088
At 31.3.1997	13982	5918	9963	-	29863

12

Drs A Brayne, C Drane and D Payne

THE EAST ROAD SURGERY

NOTES TO THE ACCOUNTS

Year Ended 31 March 1998

24.   Mortgage on Freehold Property:

The practice has a mortgage on freehold property and the loan is repayable by
Monthly instalments over 25 Years. The term of the mortgage remaining is 22
years and interest is being charged at 1.25% over bank's base rate.

25.   Capital Accounts

	A Brayne £	A Drane £	D Payne £	Total £
Property Capital:				
Balance at 1 April 1997	9300	9300	-	18600
Partner introduced:				
Transfers current account	(3100)	(3100)	6200	
	6200	6200	6200	18600
Yearly adjustments:				
Transfers current account	2500	2500	2500	7500
Balance at 31 March 1998	8700	8700	8700	26100

Represented as follows:

Freehold property at cost	183600
Less Mortgage outstanding	157500
Mortgage repaid to date	26100

	A Brayne £	A Drane £	D Payne £	Total £
Fixed Capital account:				
Balance at 1 April 1997	15000	15000	-	30000
Partner introduced:				
Transfer current account	8000	8000	23000	39000
Balance at 31 March 1998	23000	23000	23000	69000

13

Drs A Brayne   C Drane   D Payne

THE EAST ROAD SURGERY

NOTES TO THE ACCOUNTS

Year Ended 31 March 1998

25. Capital Accounts (contd.)

	A Brayne £	C Drane £	D Payne £	Total £
Current Capital:				
Balance at 1 April 1997	3527	3527	-	7054
Property revaluation	12625	12625		25250
Cash introduced	-	-	30000	30000
Partner introduced:				
Transfer fixed capital	(8000)	(8000)	(23000)	(39000)
Transfer Property capital	3100	3100	(6200)	
Bank Drawings	(10452)	(10452)	-	(20904)
	---------	---------	---------	---------
	800	800	800	2400
During the year:				
Transfer property capital	(2500)	(2500)	(2500)	(7500)
Leave advances drawn	(1500)	(1500)	(1500)	(4500)
Superann. Contributions	(6543)	(4679)	(3540)	(14762)
Bank Drawings	(38548)	(38548)	(38548)	(115644)
	---------	---------	---------	---------
	(48291)	(46427)	(45288)	(140006)
Share of net income	52366	52366	50870	* 155602
	---------	---------	---------	---------
Balance at 31 March 1998	4075	5939	5582	15596
	---------	---------	---------	---------
Summary of Capital Accounts:				
Property Capital	8700	8700	8700	26100
Fixed Capital	23000	23000	23000	69000
Current Capital	4075	5939	5582	15596
	---------	---------	---------	---------
	35775	37639	37282	110696
	---------	---------	---------	---------

* Profit share: Dr Payne's share was 51/52 x £155602/3.

14

Chapter 6

Financial Planning

Financial Planning

Small firms and professional practices often see planning as a waste of time. They would far rather be dealing with the 'real' work. However, without any planning activity at all, firms will drift along with little or no sense of purpose or direction, just reacting to the day's events, perhaps even going from one crisis to another. Partners can become disillusioned and eventually find that they are a collection of individuals whose ideas and goals no longer coincide.

The first steps in planning are not usually financial ones. What is the practice in operation to achieve? How will it achieve this? What are the short-term goals? What are the longer-term goals? Once the plan has been given some definition then it can be translated into financial terms. The plan should be reviewed at regular partners' meetings - probably held at least quarterly - and any changes necessary should be made. A proper business plan is a permanent and rolling part of the practice. It is not a document that is once written and then filed and forgotten.

Whilst it is the accountant/business manager who will assess the financial implications, the most important part of the plan is the partners' policies, and their strategy for implementing and managing those policies.

Profits are the financial end result of successful planning, although they are not the only measure of success. Partners will want to maximise their income, and profits will also be a source of funds for future development. Increased profits can also be looked upon as a sign that a practice is properly managing the resources available to it and that it is providing an efficient service to its patients. A practice which is inefficient and which is not adequately providing the services needed by its patients is not likely to be generating increased profits or even maintaining them.

Any partners cannot be described as in control of the business if they have to wait for the annual accounts to discover if they have made a profit or loss. Even more important is to know what the short-term cash requirements are. A shortage of profits is a challenge to management but no cash = no business. Even profitable businesses can go under if cash management is poor.

In the next chapter, Management Accounting, we take an in-depth look at financial planning. Much planning relies on accurate and up-to-date information from the past. In the previous chapter we examined the end of year financial statements of the East Road Surgery. Now we take another look at those figures to see what useful information can be extracted which will assist in planning future activity.

In chapter 11 are various statistics which confirm the performance of the East Road Surgery with national averages. The most useful statistics and financial ratios are those of the individual practice when they can demonstrate the changes from one accounting period to another and in helping the partners to plan for the future and to monitor how actual events conform to those which were forecast. However, it is also very useful to look at how the practice is performing in comparison to other practices and can help to identify areas of strength or weakness. These national averages are made available through the NHS Executive and through such publications as Medeconomics.

Another useful tool in financial management is the use of charts. 'A picture is worth a thousand words' so the old saying goes, and it is true that a chart will show trends much more clearly than rows of figures. Many people will find it easier to get to grips with information in this way. One of the objectives in any management reporting system is to convey the essential information to all the partners involved in the quickest and easiest way possible.

The presentation of information, whether in the form of financial statements or by way of charts, should clearly show the correlation between the data being presented and the day-to-day activities of the practice so that all partners can actively be engaged in the decision making process without having to lose too much time from patient care.

The charts in chapter 11 very easily and quickly show that the East Road Surgery has a significantly higher proportion of older patients in both age groups than the national average.

Liquidity and Cash Flow

As explained earlier it is vital for any business to maintain a healthy cash cycle. Current Assets are those assets which cycle into cash on a day-to-day basis and the Current Liabilities are those debts where the cash cycles out again at regular intervals to pay for the goods and services consumed by the practice. The first ratio we look at is the Current Ratio.

Current Ratio

The ratio of Current Assets : Current Liabilities should be higher than 2:1 so that all the current assets would be sufficient to pay off all the current liabilities. The steps to pay off creditors would be:-

Write out cheques to the value of cash held
Call in the cash owed by debtors of the practice
Sell stock on the best terms possible to generate cash
Sell some fixed assets

Usually only steps 1 and 2 are necessary. Any business that gets to step 4 so that it can pay current liabilities is usually about to go out of business.

The figures for the East Road Surgery are:

	1998	1997
Current Assets	£69120	£39179
Current Liabilities	£63162	£39488
Ratio	1.10:1	0.99:1

This shows a marginal improvement during the year but it may be regarded as unsatisfactory because the ratio is still a long way from being 2:1.

Acid Test

This is a stringent test of liquidity and is a comparison of the most liquid current assets to current liabilities:

Cash + Marketable Securities + Debtors = Current Liabilities

Stock would not be included in this test because of the time taken to convert it to cash. Prepaid expenses would also be ignored because they cannot usually be converted to cash and so they are not available to pay current liabilities.

Generally, the ratio should be at least 1:1. If the ratio falls below this then the practice may find it difficult to pay suppliers on time and the bank may be reluctant to advance short-term funds.

The East Road Surgery stock levels are not particularly high and so this ratio in their particular case is only marginally lower than the Current Ratio.

	1998	1997
Debtors and Cash	£64370	£35429
Current Liabilities	£63162	£39488
Ratio	1.02:1	0.90:1

With the bulk of GPs cash coming in regularly from the NHS, working capital and cash flow should not be the problem it is for some other businesses. However, if at any time partners drawings exceed the amount of profit being generated then the excess is effectively a withdrawal of capital - current working capital, and if this continues then cash problems will certainly occur. It is also possible for practices to try and expand too quickly with cash being diverted into fixed assets, which may take some time to start producing additional income. This cash diversion is also reducing the current working capital by converting it into fixed capital. All capital investment should be properly planned to take account of the effect on cash flow particularly in the short-term.

Liquidity

Cash & Cash Equivalents to Working Capital

	1998	**1997**
Cash	£2527	£13313
Current Liabilities	£63162	£59488
	0.04	0.34

Big reduction in 1998. East Road Surgery must be careful not to expand faster than their cash resources allows.

Cash & Marketable Securities and Receivables

Year's cash expenses

	1998	**1997**
Debtors & Cash	£64370	£35429
Expenditure exc Depreciation	£320420	£247979
	0.20	0.14
needs to be higher than	0.08	0.08
Cash expenses for one month	£26702	£20665
The ratio is	2.4:1	1.7:1
per day	£878	£679
days in hand	73	52

This shows that The East Road Surgery's liquid assets will cover 73 days of operations with cash expenses averaging £878 per day. This is an improvement over the previous year when there was the equivalent of 52 days cash expenses in hand.

It should be borne in mind that cash expenses **do not include** partners' drawings. If these are included at Y.E. 31.3.1998 levels (£115,644) the days-in-hand cover falls to 54 days (1997: 36 days).

Chapter 7

Management Accounting and Business Decisions

Management Accounting

We have seen that financial accounting was concerned with historical information, i.e. information on what had already happened. In this case the information was prepared for external parties and therefore it had to conform with generally accepted accounting principles.

However, management accounting is concerned with present and future information. Here, the information is produced for internal purposes, i.e. the management of the practice. It is to do with preparation and presentation of information in such a way as to assist management in planning, controlling and decision making. Planning means budgeting, control means comparing planned and actual performance, and decision making is choosing from among alternative courses of action for the future.

Apart from budgeting, costing is also an important part of management accounting. Services have to be costed and controlled. Information is necessary for evaluation of profitability, management efficiency and for comparison purposes. Hence, management needs such information on which to base its decisions.

Business Decisions in General Medical Practice

GPs are independent contractors with the NHS and therefore they are regarded as self-employed medical practitioners. This suggests that they operate their practices as in a free market economy. However, this is not true as the HA imposes strict control over them and the fees are not paid by the patients but the NHS. Therefore, the equilibrium pricing policy does not work in this context.

Although the NHS regulates GPs, there are ways for practices to be managed in a business like manner. Medical practices need to plan, organise and control their activities in order to achieve their goals. Decisions have to be made to minimise the costs and seek a satisfactory level of income. Hence, information is vital to the role of management.

Information relating to direct patient care and health promotion activity assists GPs to organise and decide on how such services can be provided most effectively and most efficiently. GPs have to work on face to face contact with their patients, identifying and treating illnesses. They have to manage their time most productively in order to maximise their income. Some tasks can only be handled by GPs but other tasks may be delegated to the most appropriate staff. Some nurses can handle optional clinic sessions such as asthma, diabetes, well person clinic and cervical smear tests. Other nurses can carry out delegated routine work such as dressing wounds, ear syringing and taking samples.

Income Behaviour

Here, we are concerned with finding out how income may vary with changes in the level of activity, in other words income behaviour pattern.

Direct patient care

Within a practice, income tends to follow the following pattern:
(a)   it tends to remain constant, within a range of time, regardless of the level of activity,   i.e. fixed component.
  (i)   BPA is fixed at its minimum qualifying list of 400 patients
  (ii) Maximum BPA is fixed for 1200 patients or more

In the diagram, GP1, GP2 and GP3 are Drs Brayne, Drane and Payne.

Basic Practice Allowances

(b) it tends to vary but not in direct proportion with the number of patients on the list, within the range of time, regardless of the level of activity, i.e. semi variable component.
BPA list size range from 400 to 1200 patients.

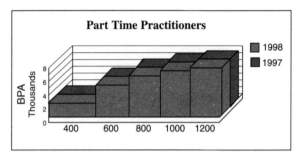

(c) it tends to vary with the number of patients, within a range of time, regardless of the level of activity i.e. variable component
Capitation varies directly with the number of patients. The steepness of the curve is dependent upon the ages of the patients. The diagram shows the fees from 1 April 1998.

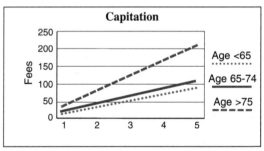

(d) it tends to vary with the number of patients and level of activity, within a range of time i.e. variable component
Item of service fees

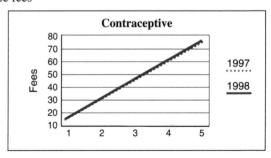

Optional Services

These are the mix of services offered by a practice. The pattern depends upon how the services are offered and managed. The practice which offers services on a reactive basis will encounter problems of efficiency and control. However, the outcome will be more predictable if the practice planned and controlled its activities. Information is the key to increasing earnings. Properly managed practices will target those areas in which there are high contributions. The chance of success will depend upon the attitude of the partners towards the management of such services.

Costing in General Medical Practice

GPs are in a service business offering their patients the use of their personal skills. They carry out a number of activities on the same principle of costing as in any other business. In medical practice, cost per patient will be the cost unit and costs have to be broken down into the cost centres.

Cost Behaviour

Within a medical practice, costs tend to follow the following pattern:

(a) Fixed Costs:
     they tend to remain constant, regardless of the level of activity.
     Rates and water, insurance, repairs and maintenance,
     depreciation, etc are expenses, which do not depend on the level of
     activity.

(b) Step costs:
     They tend to vary with the level of activity but not in a direct way that
     variable costs do.
     Light and heat, telephone, etc where the fixed element is the standing charge
     and the variable element is charge per unit/call.

(c) Variable costs:
     They tend to vary in direct proportion with the level of activity.
     Medical supplies.

Contribution approach

We have seen that costs can be classified according to their behaviour. Having analysed costs, we notice that in the short term, within a given range of activity, fixed costs will not change. We also find that by deducting the variable costs from the income, it gives a fund or contributions towards the fixed costs.

Income - Variable Costs = Contributions

Some work may have higher contributions than the others. Primary care has to be addressed but the secondary care needs to be evaluated in terms of contributions.

Optional services are activity based. It is assumed that costs are incurred by the activities required to produce the practice's services. It is based on cost per unit (or patient). It involves decisions as to which cost drivers, and how many of each, are used to make up each fully delivered service.

Example, a vaccine costs £3.75, 3.6 minutes of nursing time is taken up in a clinical activity @ 0.194p and other incidental costs of 0.15p per patient are incurred. Therefore, the variable cost per patient works out to £4.60p Vaccination fee is £5.75, reimbursement of employee cost is 0.49p and prescription issuing fee is 0.98p. Therefore, the contribution is as follows:
Income £7.22 - Variable cost £4.60 = Contribution £2.62
This means that from this activity, 1000 patients would contribute £2620 towards the overheads of the practice.

A doctor's rate is 0.713p per minute and a qualified nurse's rate is 0.194p per minute. This means that if the doctor carried out this activity, then the contributions per patient would drop from £2.62 to 0.26p per patient. In this example, income from an optional clinic session does not appear to be attractive if performed by a GP. However, if a qualified nurse carried out this activity, than it becomes economic; and contributes extra income to the practice.

Workings:

Nurse costs $\dfrac{£18699}{46 \text{ wks} \times 35 \text{ hrs}}$ = £11.62/60 min. = 0.194p per minute.

Employee cost reimbursement   0.194 x 3.6 min. x 70% = 0.49p

	Doctor	Nurse
	£	£
Vaccine fee	5.75	5.75
Prescription issuing fee	0.98	0.98
Reimbursement	-	0.49
	-------	-------
	6.73	7.22
	------	-------

Doctor's rate: £42.76/60min. = 0.713p. per min.

	Doctor	Nurse
Time taken 3.6 min. Therefore, cost is	2.57	
Nurse rate 3.6 min x 0.194		0.70
Incidental costs	0.15	0.15
Vaccine costs	3.75	3.75
	-------	-------
	6.47	4.60
	-------	-------
Contributions	0.26	2.62
	-------	-------

Time Management

Some patients may be over demanding and waste a great deal of GP's time. It will be better if a qualified nurse manages the patients when appropriate. Some patients may require time-consuming investigations and therefore be referred to a specialist at the earliest.

GPs can utilise their time most effectively by way of delegation. They can increase the practice income from the time saved by

(a) performing either higher rate work or
(b) avoiding costs of employing locums/deputies.

(a) Each hour of GP's time saved, increases contributions as follows:

Increase in contributions due to delegation of work to qualified nurse

	£
Cost of GP - Cost of a qualified nurse =	
42.76 - 3.49 =	39.27
Higher rate work undertaken	50.00

	89.27
Less value of time saved	42.76

Additional contributions per hour per GP	46.51

(b) Say, each hour of GP's time saved, would avoid costs of employing:
  - a locum costing around £33.50 per hour
  - a deputy costing around £24.50 per hour
  - a clinical assistant costing around £19.50 per hour

Financial Data:

Average total hours worked by a GP are just over 39 hours per week, excluding on call work.

Activity	Hours per week	% Time spent on activity In normal working hours
Patients contact	27.45	70%
Patient administration	5.10	13%
Practice administration	3.14	8%
Other GMS Work	2.35	6%
Non GMS such as statutorily obliged to complete documents	1.17	3%
	39.21	100%

	1.4.98	**1.12.97**
Intended Average Gross Income	£70413	£69035

Source: DDRB 27th Report 1998

GPs time may be costed as follows:

$$\text{Rate per hour} \quad \frac{I\,A\,G\,I}{42 \text{ wks* } \times 39.21 \text{ hrs}} =$$

	1.4.98	**1.12.97**
(Rate per hour)	£42.76	£41.92
Practice Nurse	£18699	£17822

$$\text{Rate per hour} \quad \frac{\text{Employee Cost}}{46 \text{ wks* } \times 35} \times 0.30^{**}$$

	1.4.98	**1.12.97**
	£3.49	£3.32

Note: * Net of Holidays ** 70% reimbursed

Locum cost: Rate per hour	£30.50 to £ 33.50	£27.00 to £30.00
Deputies: Rate per hour	£18.50 to £24.50	£16.75 to £24.50
Clinical assistant: Rate per hour	£19.50	£18.50

IAGI - Intended Average Gross Income.

Chapter 8

Budgets in Medical Practice

Budget in Medical Practice

A budget is a plan of allocated quantity and/or monetary values for a period of time. A budget forecast is a plan, prepared in advance, allocating the expected quantity and/or monetary values, for a chosen period. It is a managerial tool often used for planning and controlling the activities of the practice. Planning means setting objectives in writing and the practice directs its activities towards the ends specified in the objectives. The targets are in effect the practice's financial plan. Controlling means measuring actual performance against the expected, and corrective action is taken. A medical practice ought to prepare its budget at the beginning of the new financial year. The purpose is to improve the practice's financial position; i.e. reducing costs and raising net income.

Cash Budget

The cash budget is a financial plan allocating a practice's cash resources, based on a forecast for the future. Cash budgeting is of vital importance to practice management. It is important because it reveals not only the amount of financing but its timing as well. Where shortages of cash are known well in advance, arrangement can be made for an overdraft facility and/or negotiation of a bank loan; whereas the knowledge of excess cash can be useful in investment decisions.

Budget preparation.

The General Medical Practitioner Remuneration package is announced by the Secretary of State for Health every year in advance. When preparing a budget for the practice, the first thing to establish is:

(1)   Income paid as of right to all GPs - practice allowances and reimbursements. Hard work will not improve such income.

(2)   Income dependant on work - proper budgeting is required in this case. Statistics borrowed from various sources can be applied to evaluate the figures. National averages, profit watch fee averages, recent past experience and so on provide vital data in budget preparation for the following year.

Expenditure budgets are not difficult to prepare. The estimated figures are based on recent past experience (previous year's accounts), individual practitioner and general economic situation.

Chapter 9

Preparatory work to Budgets

The East Road Surgery **Budget Forecast**

		SR			Budget 3 mths to 30.6.98 £	Budget 3 mths to 30.9.98 £	Budget 2 mths to 30.11.98 £	Budget 4 mths to 31.3.99 £
Note:1								
Practice Allowances:								
BPA	**Note: 2a**				7584	7584	5056	10368
Seniority	**Note: 2b**	100%			1468	1467	979	1993
PGA	**Note: 2c**				2400	2400	1600	3260
Out of Hours	**Note: 2d**				2200	2200	1467	2993
Registrar Scheme	**Note: 2e**	100%			1305	1305	870	1775
Total 60274					14957	14956	9972	20389

			Actual					
Note 3		National	31.3.98					
Age		Average %	No.	%	No.	No.	No.	No.
0 - 65		84.4	6154	76.8	6410	6570	6735	6900
65 - 74		8.4	1034	12.9	985	1010	1035	1060
75 +		7.2	825	10.3	820	840	860	885
Total			8013		8215	8420	8630	8845
New Registration					202	205	210	215

The surgery has elderly patients in higher proportion than the national average.

			3 mths to 30.6.98	3 mths to 30.9.98		2 mths to 30.11.98		4 mths to 31.3.99
Capitation: Note: 4		Rate £	Amount £	Amount £	Rate £	Amount £	Rate £	Amount £
Std Capitation < 65		4.075	26121	26773	2.717	18299	5.550	38295
Std Capitation 65-74		5.388	5307	5442	3.592	3718	7.317	7756
Std Capitation >74		10.413	8539	8747	6.942	5970	14.167	12538
Sub total			39967	40962		27987		58589
Deprivation Fees: Note: 5								
Area 1			1998	2049		2100		2771
Area 2			1500	1539		1577		2190
Area 3			1148	1178		1207		1691
Sub total (25% of capitation)			4646	4766		4884		6652
Registration Note: 3 & 6 7.200			1454	1476		1512	7.350	1580
Sub total			1454	1476		1512		1580
NOTE 7 & 8								
Child Health Surveill.			1355	1390		950		1946
(0.66x no. of patients x no. of mths/12)								
Sub total			1355	1390		950		1946
Total £200116			47422	48594		35333		68767

Explanation to the Budget Forecast

(1) **Specific headings used for allocation -**

The change in rates of the Statement of Fees and Allowances come into effect as from 1 December 1998 and the periods are allocated accordingly.

(a) Budget for periods ending 30/6/98, 30/9/98, and 30/11/98 are headed to coincide with the Statement of Fees and Allowances from 1/4/98 to 30/11/98.

(b) Budget for period ending 31/3/99 is headed to coincide with the Statement of Fees and Allowances from 1/12/98 to 31/3/99.

(2) Practice allowances are limiting factors and the maximum amounts are provided in the Statement of Fees and Allowances. There are 4 partners in the budgeted year.

	From 1.4.1998	From 1.12.1998
(a) BPA	£7584/12 mths = £632 pm	£7776/12 mths = £648 pm

Multiply by 4 partners and number of months in a period.

(b) Seniority 1st Level	£470/12 mths = £39.16 pm	£480/12 mths = £40.00 pm
2nd Level	£2465/12 mths = £205.42 pm	£2510/12 mths = £209.17 pm

Multiply each level by 2 partners and number of months in a period.

(c) PGA	£2400/12 mths = £200 pm	£2445/12 mths = £203.75 pm

Multiply by 4 partners and number of months in a period.

(d) Out of Hours	£2200/12 mths = £183.33 pm	£2245/12 mths = £187.08 pm

Multiply by 4 partners and number of months in a period.

(e)	Registrar Scheme £5220/12 mths = £435 pm	£5328/12 mths = £444 pm

Multiply by the number of months in a period.

The East Road Surgery **Budget Forecast**

	Note:1	Budget 3 mths to 30.6.98 £	Budget 3 mths to 30.9.98 £	Budget 2 mths to 30.11.98 £	Budget 4 mths to 31.3.99 £	SR
Practice Allowances:						
BPA	**Note: 2a**	7584	7584	5056	10368	
Seniority	**Note: 2b**	1468	1467	979	1993	100%
PGA	**Note: 2c**	2400	2400	1600	3260	
Out of Hours	**Note: 2d**	2200	2200	1467	2993	
Registrar Scheme	**Note: 2e**	1305	1305	870	1775	100%
Total	60274	14957	14956	9972	20389	

3. The Case Study states that there is a population growth in the area and the practice expects the increase in the number of patients by 10% during the year to 31 March 1999.

Average no. of patients (net) registration and allocation forecast:

At the end of:	3mths to 31/3/98	3 mths to 30/6/98	3 mths to 30/9/98	2 mths to 30/11/98	4 mths to 31/3/99
No. of patients	8013	8215	8420	8630	8845
Increase: 10%		802	822	842	863
New Registrations: 25%		202	205	210	215

Further, it is expected that the new registrations will be allocated in accordance with the previous year trend of patients' age (Actual 31/3/98).

(4) Capitation varies directly with the number of patients. The rates are worked out as follows:

	Age	From 1.4.1998	From 1.12.1998
Std. Capitation	< 65	£16.30/12 = £1.3583 pm	£16.65/12 = £1.3875 pm
Std. Capitation	65 - 74	£21.55/12 = £1.7958 pm	£21.95/12 = £1.8292 pm
Std Capitation	> 74	£41.65/12 = £3.4708 pm	£42.50/12 = £3.5417 pm

Multiply by the number of patients at the period end and the number of months.

Note: 3

Age	National Average %	Actual 31.3.98 No.	Actual 31.3.98 %	Budget 30.6.98 No.	Budget 30.9.98 No.	Budget 30.11.98 No.	Budget 31.3.99 No.
0 - 65	84.4	6154	76.8	6410	6570	6735	6900
65 - 74	8.4	1034	12.9	985	1010	1035	1060
75 +	7.2	825	10.3	820	840	860	885
Total		8013		8215	8420	8630	8845
New Registration				202	205	210	215

The surgery has elderly patients in higher proportion than the national average.

		3 mths to 30.6.98	3 mths to 30.9.98	2 mths to 30.11.98		4 mths to 31.3.99	
Capitation: Note: 4		Rate £	Amount £	Amount £	Rate £	Amount £	Rate £	Amount £
Std Capitation	< 65	4.075	26121	26773	2.717	18299	5.550	38295
Std Capitation	65-74	5.388	5307	5442	3.592	3718	7.317	7756
Std Capitation	>74	10.413	8539	8747	6.942	5970	14.167	12538
Sub total			39967	40962		27987		58589

5.   According to the case study, 25% of the patients are recognised as being deprived.

Deprivation fees are worked out as follows:

	3 mths to 30/6/98	3 mths to 30/9/98	2 mths to 30/11/98	4 mths to 31/3/98
No. of patients	8417	8625	8840	9060
Deprivation say	2102	2156	2210	2265

	Rate £	No.	£	No.	£	No.	Rate £	No.	£
Area 1	2.85	701	1998	719	2049	737	2100 3.67	755	2771
Area 2	2.14	701	1500	719	1539	737	1577 2.90	755	2190
Area 3	1.64	700	1148	718	1178	736	1207 2.24	755	1691
		2102	4646	2156	4766	2210	4884		2265	6652

6.

	From 1.4.1998	From 1.12.1998
Registration fees	£7.20	£7.35

Multiply by the number of new patients in each period.

7.   Child Health Surveillance:

	30/6/98	30/9/98	30/11/9	31/3/99
No. of patients	8215	8420	8630	8845

Use statistics - Year ended 31/3/98 0.66p per patient - the best figure for CHS in the financial data.

Deprivation Fees: Note: 5		30.6.98	30.9.98	30.11.98		31.3.99
Area 1		1998	2049	2100		2771
Area 2		1500	1539	1577		2190
Area 3		1148	1178	1207		1691
Sub total(25% of capitation)		4646	4766	4884		6652
Registration						
Note: 3 & 6	7.200	1454	1476	1512	7.350	1580
Sub total		1454	1476	1512		1512
Child Health						
Surveill. Note: 7 & 8		1355	1390	950		1946
(0.66x no. of patients x no. of mths/12)						
Sub total		1355	1390	950		1946

THE EAST ROAD SURGERY

Financial Data:	National Average	Profit Watch Fee Averages	Year ended 31 March 1998	1997
Capitation Fees:				
New registrations	0.454	0.44	**0.53**	0.50
Child Health Surveillance	0.553	0.65	**0.66**	0.65
Target payments;				
Childhood Immun./Vaccin.		**1.71**	1.59	1.58
Cervical Cytology		**1.44**	1.34	1.32
Health Promotion	1.478	**1.59**	1.43	1.33
Sessional Payments:				
Minor surgery	0.613	**0.72**	0.63	0.47
Item of Service fees:				
Vacc. & Immun.	0.593	**0.72**	**0.72**	0.70
Contraceptives	1.106	**1.16**	1.10	1.08
Temporary residence	0.375	**0.40**	**0.40**	0.38
Emergency & Immediate				
Treatment	0.079	0.06	**0.11**	0.09
Night visits	**1.640**	1.62	**1.64**	1.57
Maternity	1.502	**1.66**	1.60	1.48
	--------	--------	--------	--------
	8.393	12.17	11.75	11.15
	--------	--------	--------	--------

National average : Source: NHS Executive
Profit Watch - Source: Medeconomics Database May 1998.

8. Budget forecast is prepared in advance by using the rates of classified income per patient and multiplying the number of patients in a chosen period. The rate of income derives from the statistical information such as the National Average, Profit Watch Fee Average and the practice's own year end results. The number of patients in a chosen period is evaluated from the practices own trend and experience. The East Road Surgery's current financial year performance was above National Average and this reflects in the financial data. The results are then compared with the Profit Watch Fee Averages. The best of the two rates of income per patient is then applied to the classified optional services to project the level of income to be targeted in the ensuing period.

The best rate of income per patient is highlighted in the Financial Data which is applied to the classified income in the budget forecast.

Additional statistics are worked out from the Accounts for the year ended 31 March 1998 for application to the budget forecast in the page opposite.

	1998 Accounts showed	No. of patients		Rate
Pre School Booster	£2728	8013		£0.34
Chronic Disease	£9133	8013		£1.14
Health Promotion average rate			£1.59	
Less Chronic disease			£1.14	£0.45
Intra Uterine Device	£3756	8013		£0.47
Emergency Treatment	£1133	8013		£0.14
Immediate Treatment	£596	8013		£0.07

The East Road Surgery	Budget Forecast (ctd)			
	3 mths to 30.6.98	3 mths to 30.9.98	2 mths to 30.11.98	4 mths to 31.3.99
No. of patients: Note: 3	8215	8420	8630	8845
	£	£	£	£
Target payments: Note: 8				
Childhood Immun./Vaccin.*	3512	3600	2460	5042
(1.71x no. of patients x no. of mths/12)				
Pre School Boosters*	698	716	489	1002
(0.34x no. of patients x no. of mths/12)				
Cervical cytology*	4732	3031	2071	4246
(1.44x no. of patients x no. of mths/12)				
Total £31599	8942	7347	5020	10290
Chronic dis. & Health Promotion: Note: 8				
Chronic disease manag.	2341	2400	1640	3361
(1.14x no. of patients x no. of mths/12)				
Health Promotion	924	947	647	1327
(0.45x no. of patients x no. of mths/12)				
Total £13587	3265	3347	2287	4688
Sessional Payments: Note: 8				
Minor surgeries	1479	1516	1036	2123
(0.72x no. of patients x no. of mths/12)				
Total £6154	1479	1516	1036	2123
Item of Service: Note: 8				
Vaccin. & Immunisation	1479	1516	1036	2123
(0.72x no. of patients x no. of mths/12)				
Contraceptives	2382	2442	1668	3420
(1.16x no. of patients x no. of mths/12)				
Intra Uterine Device	965	989	676	1386
(0.47x no. of patients x no. of mths/12)				
Temporary Residence	822	842	575	1179
(0.40x no. of patients x no. of mths/12)				
Emergency Treatment	288	294	201	413
(0.14x no. of patients x no. of mths/12)				
Immediate Treatment	144	147	101	206
(0.07x no. of patients x no. of mths/12)				
Night Visits	3368	3452	2359	4835
(1.64x no. of patients x no. of mths/12)				
Maternity	3409	3494	2388	4894
(1.66x no. of patients x no. of mths/12)				
Total £53493	12857	13176	9004	18456

*SR=100%

9. The Budget Forecast is prepared in summarised form under the main headings. The income is grouped in accordance with the rate applicable for superannuation contributions (SR). SR deductions are allocated to the partners and these are only assumptions.

The East Road Surgery   **Budget Forecast (ctd)**

Summary: Note: 9		3 mths to 30.6.98 £	3 mths to 30.9.98 £	2 mths to 30.11.98 £	4 mths 31.3.99 £	Total £
Practice Allowances		14957	14956	9972	20389	60274
Capitation		47422	48594	35333	68767	200116
Target Payments		8942	7347	5020	10290	31599
Chron.Dis./Health Prom.		3265	3347	2287	4688	13587
Sessional Payments		1479	1516	1036	2123	6154
Item of Service		12857	13176	9004	18456	53493
Total		88922	88936	62652	124713	365223
Seniority		1468	1467	979	1993	5907
Registrar scheme		1305	1305	870	1775	5255
Child. Immunisation		3512	3600	2460	5042	14614
Pre School Boosters		698	716	489	1002	2905
Cervical Cytology		4732	3031	2071	4246	14080
Total 100% SR **		11715	10119	6869	14058	42761
Balance 65.5% SR		77207	78817	55783	110655	322462
**		50570	51625	36538	72479	
6% of **		62285	61744	43407	86537	
Superannuation contribution		3737	3705	2604	5192	
Dr A Brayne	32%	1196	1185	833	1661	
Dr C Drane	32%	1196	1185	833	1661	
Dr D Payne	32%	1196	1185	833	1661	
Dr E Zain	4%	149	150	105	209	
Total allocation:		3737	3705	2604	5192	
Receipts: Advance Recoveries		57000	57000	30000	90000	
Recovery of Leave		1500	1500	1000	2000	
Balance		26685	26731	29048	27521	

The East Road Surgery		Budget Forecast (ctd)			
Note: 10		3mths to 30.6.98 £	3 mths to 30.9.98 £	2 mths to 30.11.98 £	4 mths to 31.3.99 £
Reimbursements:					
Notional Rent		3186	3186	2124	4248
Rates & Water		905	905	603	1207
Practice Staff Budget		20270	20270	13513	27027
Registrar Salary		6916	6916	4611	9221
Training Costs		2023	2023	1349	2697
Computer Maintenance		840	840	560	1120
Total (Non SR)		34140	34140	22760	45520
Prescribing Drug Payments:					
Basic Prices(expenses)		4866	5353	3926	8637
Discount(5%)		-243	-268	-196	-432
Container Allowance		24	27	20	43
VAT thereon 17.5%		813	895	656	1443
Total (Non SR)		5460	6007	4406	9691
Prescribing Drug Payments:					
On Cost					
10.5% of Basic Price		511	562	412	907
Dispensing fees					
99.3% of prescriptions		461	502	369	811
Total (65.5% SR)		972	1064	781	1718
	6% of	637	697	512	1125
Superannuation contribution		40	44	32	68
Dr A Brayne	32%	13	14	10	22
Dr C Drane	32%	13	14	10	22
Dr D Payne	32%	12	14	10	21
Dr E Zain	4%	2	2	2	3
Total allocation:		40	44	32	68
Receipts: Advance Recoveries		26000	26000	13000	42000
Balance		14532	15167	14915	14861

The East Road Surgery		Budget Forecast (ctd)			
Non NHS Income:		3 mths to 30.6.98	3 mths to 30.9.98	2 mths to 30.11.98	4 mths to 31.3.99
Note: 11		£	£	£	£
Nursing Home		720	885	1015	1555
Other Services		3551	3674	973	5523
University		360	450	750	850
Police Surgeon's Fees		3500	3575	3225	2825
Sub Total		8131	8584	5963	10753
General Hospital Sch. E (NT Code)	(100% SR)	3795	3565	3335	3450
Total		11926	12149	9298	14203
Superannuation Contributions:					
Dr A Brayne	6%	228	214	200	207
Other Fees:					
Insurance Examinations		555	570	595	525
Cremations		375	495	275	255
Private Patients		1350	995	1450	1775
		2280	2060	2320	2555

10. Similarly, budget forecast is prepared for Reimbursements and prescribing Drugs Payments. Notional rent is projected at around 95% of the mortgage interest. 70% of the Practice staff budget is reimbursed. Registrar's salary and costs are reimbursed as per payroll. Purchase of drugs, are fully reimbursible (Non SR), in addition with dispensing fees (SR).

11. The information on Non NHS Income is computed from the knowledge and agreements entered into with the appropriate bodies. Dr A Brayne has provided services to the General Hospital under the Nil Tax Code. The gross income is allocated to the firm under the partnership deed.

Note: 12.

The East Road Surgery

Budget Forecast

Payroll 1998/99	Code	Gross £	Tax £	NI E'yee £	Net £	NI E'yer £
Mr S Patel: Business Manager	543H	25200	4417	2253	18530	2520
Ms E Brown: Practice Manager	419L	17000	2816	1432	12752	1699
Ms J Yong: Prac.Nurse	419L	12600	1804	995	9801	1262
Ms A Black: Prac.Nurse	419L	8400	841	563	6996	581
Ms S Cooke: Rec/Sec.	419L	6300	421	362	5517	434
Ms T Smith: Rec/Sec.	419L	6300	421	362	5517	434
Ms S Hall: Secretary	419L	6300	421	362	5517	434
Ms H Hope: Community Nurse	419L	8400	841	563	6996	581
Ms S Lane: Midwife	419L	8400	841	563	6996	581
Ms K White: Nurse	419L	8000	761	535	6704	401
Total Ancillary staff:		106900	13584	7990	85326	8927
Part time staff		13104			13104	
Overall Total Cost:		120004				8927
Registrar Salary: Dr M Lee	543H	26600	4657	2255	19688	2660
Less Superannuation Contribution	6%	1596	Allowable for Tax but not for NIC.			
		25004				

		Cost:	Reimbursed
	Gross	106900	
	Ni'yer	8927	
		115827 x 70%	81080
Registrar Salary Inc NIC.		29260	
Less Superann. Contrib.		1596	
		27664 x 100%	27664
			108744

13. The expenses are budgeted through the knowledge and experience by using percentage increases over the previous year. Schedules of motor vehicles and HP Creditor are provided.

Note 13.
The East Road Surgery   **Budget Forecast (ctd.)**

	3 mths to 30/6/98 £	3 mths to 30/9/98 £	2 mths to 30/11/98 £	4 mths to 31/3/99 £	TOTAL £
Practice Expenses:					
Drugs	4075	4235	3737	6650	18697
Medical Instruments	2695	2216	1666	2448	9025
Medical Books, Journals, etc	762	908	535	825	3030
Courses and Conferences	1485	1402	1053	1948	5888
	9017	8761	6991	11871	36640
Premises Costs:					
Rates and Water	905	905	605	1200	3615
Light and Heat	1297	1392	1075	1538	5302
Insurance	688	688	458	918	2752
Use of Home	400	400	266	534	1600
	3290	3385	2404	4190	13269
Employee Cost:					
Staff Salaries Net	24608	24607	16405	32810	98430
PAYE and NIC **Note: 12**	10018	10018	6679	13357	40072
Trainee Salary Net	4922	4922	3615	6229	19688
Training Expenses	855	855	570	1140	3420
Locum Fees	1925	3115	2225	4445	11710
Staff Welfare	1445	1240	805	1610	5100
	43773	44757	30299	59591	178420
Administration Expenses:					
Printing and Stationery	365	345	255	505	1470
Postage and Couriers	355	405	265	525	1550
Subscriptions	1145	1145	765	1525	4580
Telephone and Mobile	1435	1795	1200	2225	6655
Cleaning and Laundry	605	615	405	815	2440
	3905	4305	2890	5595	16695
Repair and Maintenance:					
Building Repairs	2865	1165	450	2045	6525
Equipment Repairs	1735	1570	1170	1635	6110
Computer Maintenance	840	840	560	1120	3360
	5440	3575	2180	4800	15995
Motor & Travel Expenses:					
Car Running Expenses	3000	3000	2000	4000	12000
	3000	3000	2000	4000	12000
Legal and Professional:					
Solicitors costs	250	280	220	440	1190
Accountancy fees	865	865	575	1905	4210
	1115	1145	795	2345	5400

The East Road Surgery   **Budget Forecast (ctd.)**

Mortgage on Freehold Property

Date borrowed	Repay.	Initial borrowing £	Additional borrowing £	Dr A Brayne £	Dr C Drane £	Dr D Payne £	Dr E Zain £
B/fwd	1.4.98	130200	27300	-8700	-8700	-8700	
	31.3.98	-6200	-1300	-1875	-1875	-1875	-1875
C/fwd	31.3.99	124000	26000				

Interest on Mortgage **Note 14**

Year	Rate	Balance B/fwd £	Payment £	Cumulative Principal £	Cumulative Interest £	Balance C/fwd £
1998/99	8.75%	157500	-16412	2739	13673	154761
31.3.99	Adjust		-4761	4761		-4761
		157500	-21173	7500	13673	150000

The East Road Surgery   **Budget Forecast (ctd.)**

	3 mths to 30/6/98 £	3mths to 30/9/98 £	2 mths to 30/11/98 £	4 mths to 31/3/99 £	Total £
Interest Payable:					
Bank Interest	595	717	286	572	2170
Surgery Loan Interest Note:14	3418	3418	2279	4558	13673
	4013	4135	2565	5130	15843
Other Finance Charges:					
Bank Charges	247	382	244	488	1361
H P Interest re Equip.	498	498	333	665	1994
H P Interest re Motor Vehicles	1215	1215	810	1620	4860
Equipment Leasing	0	0	0	0	0
	1960	2095	1387	2773	8215
Depreciation:					
Furniture, Fixtures and Fittings	655	655	436	876	2622
Computer Equipment	277	277	185	371	1110
Medical and Office Equipment	467	467	310	624	1868
Motor Vehicles	2480	2480	1654	3308	9922
	3879	3879	2585	5179	15522

Motor Vehicles	Dr A Brayne	Dr C Drane	Dr D Payne	Total
Acquired on 6.4.97	17640	17640	17640	52920
H P Deposit paid	-1440	-1440	-1440	-4320
Finance by H P (36 Instal.)	16200	16200	16200	48600
H P Charges	4800	4800	4800	14400
Total cost	21000	21000	21000	63000
1st Year (Y.E. 31.3.98) Cost	5400	5400	5400	16200
Int.	2400	2400	2400	7200
Repay.	7800	7800	7800	23400
2nd Year (Y.E. 31.3.99)Cost	5400	5400	5400	16200
Int.	1620	1620	1620	4860
Repay.	7020	7020	7020	21060
3rd Year (Y.E. 31.3.00)Cost	5400	5400	5400	16200
Int.	780	780	780	2340
Repay.	6180	6180	6180	18540

Chapter 10

Budgeted Forecast Statements

Explanation to the Cash Flow Forecast

The monthly cash flow forecast for the 12 months to 31 March 1999 is a budget forecast prepared in advance showing the movement of cash in and out of the medical practice. The aim is to avoid the liquidity problems such as shortage of cash well in advance and at the same time to ensure that no cash is lying idle. In order to prepare an effective forecast, reliable information is required and medical practices are in a better position than any other business in this respect. The case study forecasts are based on 1998/99 Revised Fees and Allowances payable to GPs circularised by the NHS Executive in March 1998. The East Road Surgery does not have problems with the credit control since most cash inflows - fees, allowances, reimbursements and grants, come from the HA on a regular basis. Detailed costing is carried out to provide accurate figures on the cash payments, such as expenses, drawings and capital expenditures, which outflow on a timely basis. Overall, the business manager is in control of the practice administration and this is how he is able to maintain the balanced cash flow.

Monthly cash flow forecast.

1. Opening balance on 1 April 1998 showed that the practice had overdrawn from the Bank by £6734. The practice already has an overdraft facility of £15,000.

2. Cash Inflows: Actual receipts from whatever source, revenue and/or capital during the month are shown. In April 1998, cash was received from the debtors outstanding at 31 March 1998.

3. Cash Outflows: Actual payments for whatever reason, expense, capital and/or drawings during the month is shown. In April 1998, cash was paid to the creditors outstanding at 31 March 1998.

4. Closing bank balance is arrived at by adding the opening bank balance to the total receipts and subtracting the figure for total payments. The closing bank balance is carried forward to the next month as an opening bank balance.

Summary of Cash Flow Forecast

		30.6.98 £	30.9.98 £	30.11.98 £	31.3.99 £
(2)	Cash Inflow	155595	138744	99892	189384
(3)	Cash Outflow	(153180)	(128064)	(86232)	(175141)
	Net Cash Flow	2415	10680	13660	14243
(1)	Balance B/Fwd	(6734)	(4319)	6361	20021
(4)	Balance C/Fwd	(4319)	6361	20021	34264

Monthly cash flow forecast is shown on pages to follow.

THE EAST ROAD SURGERY   **CASH FLOW FORECAST**

Note: 2	April-98 Budget	Actual	May-98 Budget	Actual	Jun-98 Budget	Actual
CASH INFLOWS :						
NHS:						
Fees and Allowances	24286*		28500		28500	
Reimbursements	32897*		10870		10870	
Prescribing Drug Payments	4660*		2130		2130	
NON NHS:						
Nursing Home	240		240		240	
Other Services						
University	120		120		120	
Police Surgeon's fees	1166		1167		1167	
General Hospital	1189		1189		1189	
OTHER FEES:						
Insurance examination	185		185		185	
Cremations	125		125		125	
Private patients	450		450		450	
Misc:						
Interest Received:					325	
TOTAL RECEIPTS	65318		44976		45301	
Note: 3						
CASH OUTFLOWS :						
Practice Expenses	3515**		3005		3006	
Premises Costs	1485**		963		1363	
Employee Cost	11251		11252		11252	
PAYE & NIC	9217**		3339		3339	
Administration Costs	1920**		1301		1302	
Repairs & Renewals	1855**		1813		1813	
Motor & Travel	1000		1000		1000	
Legal & Professional	1575**					
Bank Interest					595	
Other Finance Charges					247	
Mortgage Repayments	1367		1367		1367	
HP Repayments	2807		2807		2807	
Partners' Drawings	15000		15000		15000	
CAPITAL EXPENDITURES					17250	
TOTAL PAYMENTS	50992		41847		60341	
NET CASHFLOW	14326		3129		-15040	
Note: 1						
BALANCE B/FWD	-6734		7592		10721	
Note: 4						
BALANCE C/FWD	7592		10721		-4319	

         *Debtors   **Creditors

THE EAST ROAD SURGERY			CASH FLOW FORECAST			
	Jul-98		Aug-98		Sept-98	
Note: 2	Budget	Actual	Budget	Actual	Budget	Actual
CASH INFLOWS :						
NHS:						
Fees and Allowances	26685*		28500		28500	
Reimbursements	12401*		10658		10658	
Prescribing Drug Payments	2131*		2342		2342	
NON NHS:						
Nursing Home	295		295		295	
Other Services	3551					
University	150		150		150	
Police Surgeon's fees	1191		1192		1192	
General Hospital	1117		1117		1117	
OTHER FEES:						
Insurance examination	190		190		190	
Cremations	165		165		165	
Private patients	331		332		332	
Misc:						
Interest Received:					655	
TOTAL RECEIPTS	48207		44941		45596	
Note: 3						
CASH OUTFLOWS :						
Practice Expenses	3006**		2920		2920	
Premises Costs	964**		995		1395	
Employee Cost	11579		11580		11580	
PAYE & NIC	3340**		3339		3339	
Administration Costs	1302**		1435		1435	
Repairs & Renewals	1814**		1191		1192	
Motor & Travel	1000		1000		1000	
Legal & Professional	1115**					
Bank Interest					717	
Other Finance Charges					382	
Mortgage Repayments	1367		1368		1368	
HP Repayments	2807		2807		2807	
Partners' Drawings	15000		15000		15000	
CAPITAL EXPENDITURES						
TOTAL PAYMENTS	43294		41635		43135	
NET CASHFLOW	4913		3306		2461	
Note: 1						
BALANCE B/FWD	-4319		594		3900	
Note: 4						
BALANCE C/FWD	594		3900		6361	

*Debtors   **Creditors

THE EAST ROAD SURGERY   **CASH FLOW FORECAST**

	Oct-98		Nov-98		Dec-98	
Note: 2	Budget	Actual	Budget	Actual	Budget	Actual
CASH INFLOWS :						
NHS:						
Fees and Allowances	26731*		30000		29048*	
Reimbursements	12824*		10423		12337*	
Prescribing Drugs	2343*		2577		2578*	
NON NHS:						
Nursing home	507		508		388	
Other Services	3674				973	
University	375		375		212	
Police Surgeon's fees	1612		1613		706	
General Hospital	1567		1568		810	
OTHER FEES:						
Insurance examination	297		298		131	
Cremations	137		138		63	
Private patients	725		725		443	
Misc:						
Interest Received			875			
TOTAL RECEIPTS	50792		49100		47689	
Note: 3						
CASH OUTFLOWS :						
Practice Expenses	2921**		3495		3496**	
Premises Costs	995**		1335		1069**	
Employee Cost	11810		11810		11558	
PAYE & NIC	3340**		3339		3340**	
Administration Costs	1435**		1445		1445**	
Repairs & Renewals	1192**		1090		1090**	
Motor & Travel	1000		1000		1000	
Legal & Professional	1145**				795**	
Bank Interest			286			
Other Finance Charges			244			
Mortgage Repayments	1368		1368		1368	
HP Repayments	2807		2807		2807	
Partners' Drawings	15000		15000		15000	
CAPITAL EXPENDITURES						
TOTAL PAYMENTS	43013		43219		42968	
NET CASHFLOW	7779		5881		4721	
Note: 1						
BALANCE B/FWD	6361		14140		20021	
Note: 4						
BALANCE C/FWD	14140		20021		24742	

*Debtors **Creditors

THE EAST ROAD SURGERY			CASHFLOW FORECAST		
	Jan-99		Feb-99		March-99
Note: 2	Budget	Actual	Budget	Actual	Budget	Actual
CASH INFLOWS :						
NHS:						
Fees and Allowances	30000		30000		30000	
Reimbursements	11165		11165		11165	
Prescribing Drugs	2835		2835		2835	
NON NHS:						
Nursing home	389		389		389	
Other Services						
University	212		213		213	
Police Surgeon's fees	706		706		707	
General Hospital	811		811		811	
OTHER FEES:						
Insurance examination	131		131		132	
Cremations	64		64		64	
Private patients	444		444		444	
Misc:						
Interest Received					1420	
TOTAL RECEIPTS	46757		46758		48180	
Note: 3						
CASH OUTFLOWS :						
Practice Expenses	2967		2968		2968	
Premises Costs	914		914		1448	
Employee Cost	11558		11559		11559	
PAYE & NIC	3339		3339		3339	
Administration Costs	1398		1399		1399	
Repairs & Renewals	1200		1200		1200	
Motor & Travel	1000		1000		1000	
Legal & Professional					1155	
Bank Interest					572	
Other Finance Charges					488	
Mortgage Repayments	1368		1368		6129	
HP Repayments	2807		2807		2811	
Partners' Drawings	15000		15000		15000	
CAPITAL EXPENDITURES						
TOTAL PAYMENTS	41551		41554		49068	
NET CASH FLOW	5206		5204		-888	
Note: 1						
BALANCE B/FWD	24742		29948		35152	
Note: 4						
BALANCE C/FWD	29948		35152		34264	

Explanation of 'Link between Cash Flow and Income Statement'

This is prepared as an extended trial balance.

Debtors brought forward and carried forward are listed and agreed.

Creditors brought forward and carried forward are listed and agreed.

Cash inflow and outflow for the whole year are listed and agreed.

Adjustments are required for postings to drawings etc - leave payment, superannuation contributions, capital element of mortgage repayment and HP repayments.

Final income and expenditure totals should reconcile with the Income Statement at 31 March 1999.

EAST ROAD SURGERY **Link between Cash Flow & Income Statement**

Income:	O/S b/fwd	O/S c/fwd	Cash Sub total 6 mths to 30/9/98	Cash Sub Total 6 mths to 31/3/99	Cash Total	Adjust	Final I & E
NHS:							
Fees and Allowances	24286	-27521	175779	164971	340750	* 21238	365223
Reimbursements	32897	-12025	69079	88354	157433		136561
Prescribing Drugs	4660	-2836	16003	15735	31738	SR 84	30098
NON NHS:							
Nursing home			2570	1605	4175		4175
Other Services		-5523	4647	3551	8198		13721
University			1600	810	2410		2410
Police Surgeon's fees			6050	7075	13125		13125
General Hospital			6378	6918	13296	SR 849	14145
OTHER FEES:							
Insurance examination			1120	1125	2245		2245
Cremations			530	870	1400		1400
Private patients			3225	2345	5570		5570
Misc:							
Interest Received			2295	980	3275		3275
Total	£61843	£-47905			£583615	£22271	**£591948**

Expenditure:

	O/S b/fwd	O/S c/fwd	Cash Sub total	Cash Sub Total	Cash Total	Adjust	Final I & E
Practice Expenses	-3515	2968	18815	18372	37187		36640
Premises Costs	-1485	914	6675	7165	13840		13269
Employee Cost			69854	68494	138348		138348
PAYE & NIC	-9217	3340	20036	25913	45949		40072
Administration Costs	-1920	1399	8521	8695	17216		16695
Repairs & Renewals	-1855	1200	6972	9678	16650		15995
Motor & Travel			6000	6000	12000		12000
Legal & Professional	-1575	1190	3095	2690	5785		5400
Bank Interest			858	1312	2170		2170
Other Finance Charges			732	629	1361	**6854	8215
Mortgage Repayments			12969	8204	21173	*** -7500	13673
HP Repayments			16846	16842	33688	**** -33688	
Partners' Drawings			90000	90000	180000	-180000	
Depreciation						15522	15522
Total	£-19567	£11011			£525367	£-198812	**£317999**

Note:	*	**	***	****
	6000 Leave	1994 HP Int M/C	7500Mort. Repaid	12628 HP on M/C
	15238 SR	4860 HP Int M/V		21060 HP on M/V

Budgeted Income Statement

The budgeted Income Statement and Financial Position Statement, referred to as the Master budget, represent the summarised plans for the practice for the forthcoming period. The Income Statement, which shows the expected Income and Expenditure for the budget period, is concerned with revenue earned and expense incurred. In other words, the accounts are prepared on an accrual basis, therefore, the figures in the profit forecasts will be different from the Cash flow forecast. Cash flow is based on the movement of actual cash in and out of the practice.

THE EAST ROAD SURGERY **INCOME STATEMENT**

	3mths to 30.6.98		3mths to 30.9.98		6mths to 30.9.98	
	Forecast	Actual	Forecast	Actual	Forecast	Actual
INCOME:						
Practice Allowances	14957		14956		29913	
Capitation Fees	47422		48594		96016	
Target Payments	8942		7347		16289	
Chronic Disease Management						
and Health Promotion	3265		3347		6612	
Sessional Payments	1479		1516		2995	
Item of Service	12857		13176		26033	
NHS INCOME	88922		88936		177858	
Other NHS Payments	972		1064		2036	
Reimbursements	39600		40147		79747	
Appointments	11926		12149		24075	
Other Fees	2280		2060		4340	
TOTAL INCOME	143700		144356		288056	
EXPENDITURE:						
Practice Expenses	9017		8761		17778	
Premises Costs	3290		3385		6675	
Employee Cost	43773		44757		88530	
Administration Expenses	3905		4305		8210	
Repairs & Renewals	5440		3575		9015	
Motor Expenses	2250		2250		4500	
Travel & Subsistence	750		750		1500	
Legal & Professional	1115		1145		2260	
Interest	4013		4135		8148	
Other Finance Charges	1960		2095		4055	
Depreciation	3879		3879		7758	
TOTAL EXPENDITURE	79392		79037		158429	
NET PROFIT	64308		65319		129627	
INCOME FROM						
INVESTMENT	325		655		980	
TOTAL NET INCOME	£64633		£65974		£130607	

THE EAST ROAD SURGERY   **INCOME STATEMENT**

	6 mths to 30.9.98		2 mths to 30.11.98		8 mths to 30.11.98	
	Forecast	Actual	Forecast	Actual	Forecast	Actual
INCOME:						
Practice Allowances	29913		9972		39885	
Capitation Fees	96016		35333		131349	
Target Payments	16289		5020		21309	
Chronic Disease Management						
and Health Promotion	6612		2287		8899	
Sessional Payments	2995		1036		4031	
Item of Service	26033		9004		35037	
NHS INCOME	177858		62652		240510	
Other NHS Payments	2036		781		2817	
Reimbursements	79747		27166		106913	
Appointments	24075		9298		33373	
Other Fees	4340		2320		6660	
TOTAL INCOME	288056		102217		390273	
EXPENDITURE:						
Practice Expenses	17778		6991		24769	
Premises Costs	6675		2404		9079	
Employee Cost	88530		30299		118829	
Administration Expenses	8210		2890		11100	
Repairs & Renewals	9015		2180		11195	
Motor Expenses	4500		1500		6000	
Travel & Subsistence	1500		500		2000	
Legal & Professional	2260		795		3055	
Interest	8148		2565		10713	
Other Finance Charges	4055		1387		5442	
Depreciation	7758		2585		10343	
TOTAL EXPENDITURE	158429		54096		212525	
NET PROFIT	129627		48121		177748	
INCOME FROM						
INVESTMENT	980		875		1855	
TOTAL NET INCOME	£130607		£48996		£179603	

THE EAST ROAD SURGERY INCOME STATEMENT

	8 mths to 30.11.98		4 mths to 31.3.99		12 mths to 31.3.99	
	Forecast	Actual	Forecast	Actual	Forecast	Actual
INCOME:						
Practice Allowances	39885		20389		60274	
Capitation Fees	131349		68767		200116	
Target Payments	21309		10290		31599	
Chronic Disease Management						
and Health Promotion	8899		4688		13587	
Sessional Payments	4031		2123		6154	
Item of Service	35037		18456		53493	
NHS INCOME	240510		124713		365223	
Other NHS Payments	2817		1718		4535	
Reimbursements	106913		55211		162124	
Appointments	33373		14203		47576	
Other Fees	6660		2555		9215	
TOTAL INCOME	390273		198400		**588673**	
					Note: B	
EXPENDITURE:						
Practice Expenses	24769		11871		36640	
Premises Costs	9079		4190		13269	
Employee Cost	118829		59591		178420	
Administration Expenses	11100		5595		16695	
Repairs & Renewals	11195		4800		15995	
Motor Expenses	6000		3000		9000	
Travel & Subsistence	2000		1000		3000	
Legal & Professional	3055		2345		5400	
Interest	10713		5130		15843	
Other Finance Charges	5442		2773		8215	
Depreciation	10343		5179		15522	
TOTAL EXPENDITURE	212525		105474		**317999**	
					Note: A	
NET PROFIT	177748		92926		270674	
INCOME FROM						
INVESTMENT	1855		1420		**3275**	
					Note: B	
TOTAL NET INCOME	£179603		£94346		£273949	

Refer to 'Link between Cash Flow and Income Statement'
Note: A Total expenditure reconciled
Note: B Total income reconciled

Budgeted Financial Position Statement

This is part of the Master Budget. It is a statement of affairs summarising assets, liabilities and capital. It reflects the future position of the practice.

THE EAST ROAD SURGERY		FINANCIAL POSITION STATEMENT		
		Year ended 31 March 1999		
		Balances	Forecast	Actual
		At 1.4.98	At 31.3.99	At 31.3.99
Fixed Assets:		£	£	£
Surgery Freehold Property		208850	208850	
Furn. Fix. & Fittings	NBV	10487	10487	
Prov.for Dep'n			-2622	
Computer Equip.	NBV	4439	4439	
Prov.for Dep'n			-1110	
Office & Medical Equip.	NBV	7472	7422	
Addition			17250	
Prov.for Dep'n			-1868	
Motor Vehicles	NBV	39690	39690	
Prov.for Dep'n			-9922	
Current Assets:				
Stock		4750	4750	
Debtors		61843	47905	
Bank Deposit		2477	33275	
Bank Current			889	
Cash in Hand		50	100	
Current Liabilities:				
Bank Overdraft		-9261		
HP Creditor		-26834	-16200	
Creditors		-19567	-11011	
Long Term Liabilities:				
Mortgage on Property		-157500	-150000	
HP Creditor >1 yr.		-16200		
Partners' Property Capital:				
Dr A Brayne		-8700	-8700	
Dr C Drane		-8700	-8700	
Dr D Payne		-8700	-8700	
Dr E Zain				
Partners' Fixed Capital:				
Dr A Brayne		-23000	-23000	
Dr C Drane		-23000	-23000	
Dr D Payne		-23000	-23000	
Dr E Zain				
Partners' Current Accounts:				
Dr A Brayne		-4075	-4075	
Dr C Drane		-5939	-5939	
Dr D Payne		-5582	-5582	
Dr E Zain				
Net Income			-273949	
Drawings			180000	
SR			16271	
Leave recovery			6000	
Net Total		0	0	

Chapter 11

*Financial Analyses and
Evaluation of Performance*

Financial analyses and evaluation of performance

Once the financial or management accounts are prepared, the business manager has to convey information to the partners. He has to comment to them on the performance of various activities of the practice. In order to produce such information, he has to analyse the accounts and then reveal underlying trends in the practice's activities.

The technique used in this case is the preparation of important statistics. The financial ratios and statistical comparisons is the most important tool for interpreting the results of operation of the practice. These are the most commonly used devices for assessing the profitability and efficiency of general medical practices.

Charts are a useful device for giving a clear picture of the business situation. The most common form of diagrammatic representations are Pie diagrams and Bar charts. The Pie diagrams consist of a circle divided into sectors and each sector is proportionate to the class it represents. The Pie diagram shows how the NHS Income is allocated. The Bar charts consist of blocks as illustrated by Patients Age Charts. They are represented by the proportionate height of the blocks rather than the area.

Results of the operations and forecast

Brief comments are made on the financial data presented. Overall, the practice is performing well. There is a constant drive for efficiency of the medical practice. The average number of patients per GP has improved from 2171 to 2003. The forecast for 1999 indicate that the number will come down below the national average to 1789. Although average gross NHS Income has dropped, the efficiency drive has helped the practice to increase the average net NHS Income. Thus, the gross and net NHS income per patient has improved and forecasts indicate further improvements in 1999. Other Non NHS activities are on the increasing trend. The practice is watchful of the abatement rule. The forecasted income includes income from public sources and therefore, private proportion comprises less than 10%.

ALLOCATION OF GROSS NHS INCOME

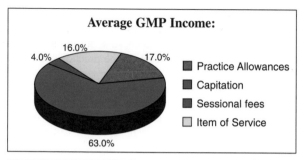

Average GMP Income:

- Practice Allowances
- Capitation
- Sessional fees
- Item of Service

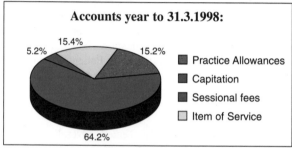

Accounts year to 31.3.1998:

- Practice Allowances
- Capitation
- Sessional fees
- Item of Service

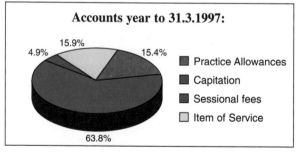

Accounts year to 31.3.1997:

- Practice Allowances
- Capitation
- Sessional fees
- Item of Service

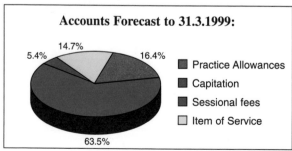

Accounts Forecast to 31.3.1999:

- Practice Allowances
- Capitation
- Sessional fees
- Item of Service

THE EAST ROAD SURGERY

Financial Data:	Average GP's Income	Year ended 31 March.		
		1998	1997	1999 Forecast
Allocation of gross NHS Income:	%	%	%	%
Practice allowances	17	15.2	15.4	16.4
Capitation fees incl. Target payments	63	64.2	63.8	63.5
Sessional fees & Health Promotion	4	5.2	4.9	5.4
Item of service fees	16	15.4	15.9	14.7
	-------	-------	-------	-------
	100	100.0	100.0	100.0
	-------	-------	-------	-------

Average GPs Income - Source: GP Handbook BMA by Norman Ellis 1997

The statistical comparisons above indicates the following:

- the firm has higher capitation fees than the national average due to higher than average number of patients on the partnership list.
- health promotional activity is on a higher level than the national average.
- item of service fees require improvement.
- practice allowances are fixed amounts; they are not work dependant and therefore, proportionally reducing as other income is improving.

Gross NHS Income

The financial data indicates that Gross NHS Income for 1998 has increased by 8.39% over 1997. Income per patient has also increased from £36.76 (1997) to £39.84 (1998). 24.91% of the total increase in Gross NHS Income was due to the merger of Dr Payne's practice.

Budgeted Accounts 1999

Income per patient has been budgeted at a modest increase of 3.64% over 1998. Around 10.78% further increase will be expected due to the increase in the number of patients. Overall increase is expected to be 14.42%.

THE EAST ROAD SURGERY

Financial Data:		For the years ended	
	1997 (Actual)	1998 (Actual)	1999 (Forecast)
Gross NHS Income	£239523	£319205	£365223
No. of patients	6515	8013	8845
Per patient	£36.76	£39.84	£41.29

Explanation towards the changes in Gross NHS Income:

Year ended 31 march 1998:   £

Percent increase over 1997 (39.84 - 36.76/36.76)	20002	8.39%
Percent increase due to merger: (1498 patients x 39.84)	59680	24.91%
Overall increase	79682	33.30%

Year ended 31 March 1999 (Forecast):

	£	
Percent increase over 1998 (41.29 - 39.84/39.84)	11665	3.64%
Percent increase due to increase in number of patients (832 patients x 42.91)	34353	10.78%
Overall increase	46018	14.42%

PATIENTS AGE CHARTS

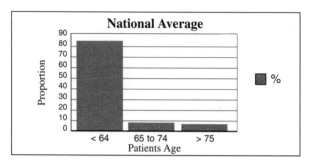

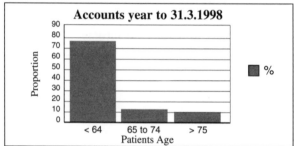

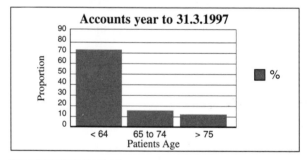

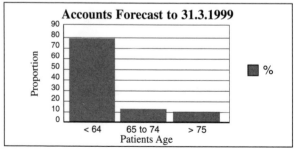

THE EAST ROAD SURGERY

Financial Data: Patients age	National Average 1997/98 %	1998 %	Year ended 31 March No.	1997 %	No.	1999 (Forecast) %	No.
0 - 64	84.4	76.8	6154	73.5	4789	78.0	6900
65 - 74	8.4	12.9	1034	14.8	964	12.0	1060
75 and over	7.2	10.3	825	11.7	762	10.0	885
	100.0	100.0	8013	100.0	6515	100.0	8845
Partners			3		2		4
Average patients per partner			2671		3257		2211
Full time GPs			4		3		5
Average patients per GP	1881		2003		2171		1789

National average - Source: GMS Statistics(1997) & Compendium of Health Statistics 10th Edit.

Financial Data: Gross NHS Income (exclude reimbursements):	Intended Income £	1998 £	Year ended 31 March 319205	1997 £ 239523	1999 (Forecast) £ 365223
per full partner		106402		119762	91306
per GP	69035	79801		79841	73045
per patient	36.70	39.84		36.76	41.29
Net NHS Income:		284295		213259	328583
Per full partner		94765		106629	109528
Per GP	46450	71074		71086	65717
Per patient	24.70	35.48		32.73	37.15

Intended Income - Source: NHS Executive March 1998.

The statistics on the opposite page indicate how the practice performed during 1997 and 1998. The results are compared with outside statistics. Target payments and Health promotion performed below average during 1997 and 1998. There is a need for improvement here. Overall, the practice results are above National Average but just under Profit Watch Fee Averages.

Projection of trends into the future.

Preparatory work to budgets - chapter 9 note 8 explains how the budget forecast is prepared using the statistical information such as the best rates of classified income per patient. The financial data shows income per patient comparatives of National Average, Profit Watch Fee Average and latest practice year-end results.

THE EAST ROAD SURGERY

Financial Data:	National Average	Profit Watch Fee Averages	Year ended 31 March 1998	1997
Capitation Fees:				
New registrations	0.454	0.44	0.53	0.50
Child Health Surveillance	0.553	0.65	0.66	0.65
Target payments;				
Childhood Immun./Vaccin.		1.71	1.59	1.58
Cervical Cytology		1.44	1.34	1.32
Health Promotion	1.478	1.59	1.43	1.33
Sessional Payments:				
Minor surgery	0.613	0.72	0.63	0.47
Item of Service fees:				
Vacc. & Immun.	0.593	0.72	0.72	0.70
Contraceptives	1.106	1.16	1.10	1.08
Temporary residence	0.375	0.40	0.40	0.38
Emergency & Immediate Treatment	0.079	0.06	0.11	0.09
Night visits	1.640	1.62	1.64	1.57
Maternity	1.502	1.66	1.60	1.48
	--------	--------	--------	--------
	8.393	12.17	11.75	11.15
	--------	--------	--------	--------

National average : Source: NHS Executive
Profit Watch - Source: Medeconomics Database May 1998.

The financial data for other activities of the practice shows an overall increase from £12038 (1997) to £34373 (1998). This is mainly due to time management. The partners are utilising their time most effectively by way of delegation. Most of the income is derived from public services. The ratio of other activities to total income indicates increase in proportion from 4.79% (1997) to 9.72% (1998). The 1999 forecast predicts that the proportion will increase to 14.38%.

THE EAST ROAD SURGERY

Financial Data:	For the year ended		
	Actual	Actual	Forecast
	1997	1998	1999
Other activities:			
	£	£	£
Dispensing	1948	2924	4535
General Hospital	2225	12164	14145
University	-	1170	2410
Police Surgeon's Report	2676	11525	13125
Nursing Homes	2672	2810	4175
Insurance	1322	1985	2245
Cremation	129	195	1400
Private Patients	1066	1600	5570
Other Services	-	-	13721
	---------	---------	---------
	12038	34373	61326
	---------	---------	---------
NHS Income	239523	319205	365223
	---------	---------	---------
Total Income	251561	353578	426549
	---------	---------	---------
Other Activities: Total Income	**4.79%**	**9.72%**	**14.38%**

Chapter 12

Taxation

Taxation Aspects

> "..........in this world nothing is certain but death and taxes."
> (Benjamin Franklin, 1789)

This is still an oft-repeated phrase two hundred years later. Despite the inevitability of both, we still try to avoid them if we can.

Taxation in all its many guises has become a very extensive and complex subject. Although this book is essentially focused on the accounting aspects of general practice, it was considered appropriate to include a chapter explaining the basic concepts as they affect general practice. As with any specialist subject, there is no substitute for consulting an expert in specific situations and we recommend that you do this. Hopefully, the following information will give you a basic grounding in understanding what the expert tells you.

Self-assessment is now with us and the examples in the case study are dealt with in this context. There were transitional provisions for 'old' businesses (i.e. those that were in operation prior to 6 April 1994 and continued past 6 April 1996) which had a big impact on the 1996/97 tax year, the first year of self-assessment. Since this year is now behind us, these transitional provisions are not covered here. It should be mentioned, however, that there are anti-avoidance transitional provisions that rumble through 1997/98 and 1998/99 in respect of cessations during those years.

The self-assessment system puts the burden of record keeping, making returns, and calculating the amount due, with the taxpayer. The Inland Revenue's role is now that of processing the return, collecting the tax due and policing the system. Penalties can be imposed on the taxpayer for non-compliance. General Practitioners are usually employers as well and so have the additional responsibility of being a tax collection point for the government under the Pay As You Earn system. Again, penalties are imposed if you get it wrong or miss the time limits.

Pay As You Earn

All practice employees come within the scope of the PAYE system. Even part time employees whose remuneration is below the National Insurance starting levels may still be liable to tax deductions. Any employee who does not produce a form P45 at the commencement of the employment is required to complete a form P46. It is the employee's responsibility to let you know if their circumstances change but it is best practice to renew the P46 declarations at the beginning of each new tax year for the relevant employees.

Pay also includes taxable benefits. Benefits must be declared at the end of each tax year on form P11D for 'higher' paid employees (Higher paid in Inland Revenue terms is anything above £8,500 p.a. including benefits.) or form P9D for other employees. It may be possible to avoid some of the paperwork by arranging a dispensation with your local tax office to cover certain expenses, e.g. an employee's mileage allowance. During the tax year the deductions made from employees' pay together with employer's National Insurance Contributions must be paid over to the Inland Revenue at the end of each tax month. (These begin on 6th April and end on 5th of each month.) Payments may be made quarterly if the amounts due on average do not exceed £600 per month. At the end of each tax year the Employer's Annual Return forms must be completed and sent back to the Inland Revenue within a specified time limit and fixed penalties can be imposed if these are missed. From April 1999 the Contributions Agency will become part of the Inland Revenue. This should help administration on both sides. It will also put the inspection of records completely in the hands of the Inland Revenue.

Statutory Sick Pay (SSP) and Statutory Maternity Pay (SMP) are also the responsibility of the employer to administer and some of the burden of cost has also passed to the employer. When producing budgets and forecasts it must be remembered that the cost of employing somebody is not just the amount of their gross pay but also the employer's NIC, benefits in kind, and possibly some SSP/SMP costs as well. Although the majority of this will be reimbursed by the NHS, it will have an effect on cash flow. The procedures for reimbursement are set out in the 'Red Book', and even more clearly in 'Making Sense Of The Red Book' by Norman Ellis and John Chisholm (Radcliffe Medical Press).

Record Keeping

Prior to 6 April 1996 it was not a legal requirement to keep records for tax purposes. From a practical point of view, those people who did not were asking for trouble and often got it when chosen for a tax enquiry. From 6 April 1996 it is now a legal requirement to keep proper records. For GP's these should not be a problem because proper record keeping is already part and parcel of being in practice. However, with penalties of up to £3,000 on offer it is worth looking at some specific items.

Tax deductible expenses are those which are incurred wholly and exclusively in earning the fee income. The wages of a nurse and the cost of lighting and heating a surgery clearly fall into this category. The expenses would not be incurred if there were no practice. However, items such as car running expenses and home telephone have a dual purpose - both business and private use. Those expenses are apportioned but proper records must be kept to show the basis of the apportionment. Just picking a figure out of the air - 'say 20% private use' - will not do.

Motor Expenses

Travelling between home and work is not allowable since such expenses are not incurred in carrying on the medical practice. The expenses incurred in visiting patients, travelling to and from seminars and conferences, and any other trip on practice related business is deductible for tax purposes. A GP should keep a logbook for recording business mileage, the total overall mileage for the year and record fuel costs, repairs and servicing, road tax, insurance, subscriptions to AA/RAC etc.

Spouses Salary

The cost of employing a GP's spouse in the medical practice is allowable for tax purposes if it can be shown that the spouse is providing assistance in the running of the practice and that the wages paid are the going market rate. If the spouse undertakes duties which justify a higher salary then the spouse should be rewarded accordingly. The spouse is in fact in the same position as any other employee of the practice as regards tax and NIC thresholds etc. (see the Pay As You Earn section, *ante*).

Business use of Home

The cost of accommodation is apportioned between business and domestic use. A GP may use a room at home for patient consultation, or as a study or for administrative work. The claim is usually made in relation to the total number of rooms and will include a proportion of lighting, heating, cleaning, repairs and decorating, security costs, council tax. Capital Allowances can be claimed on items of capital expenditure such as desk, chairs, filing cabinets, etc. if these are used for the medical practice business even though they are situated at home. It is also possible to claim tax relief on a proportion of mortgage interest payable where part of the home is used for the purposes of the medical practice.

Self Assessment

The tax year 1996/97 (6 April 1996 to 5 April 1997) was the first year of the self-assessment tax system. In theory this means that the taxpayer will complete a tax return, calculate the tax liability and make the payment to the Inland Revenue. In practice, many taxpayers will continue to have their tax returns completed by agents; for tax returns submitted by 30 September each year, the Inland Revenue will do the calculations, instead of the taxpayer; and the Inland Revenue will issue Statements of Account to show the amount due, together with a tear-off payslip. In fact the Inland Revenue will continue to make the calculations even after the 30 September but cannot guarantee to be able to provide the information before the payment deadline of 31 January. The onus under self-assessment is with the taxpayer to make sure that full and complete returns are filed on time and that the proper amounts due are paid on time.

A sole practitioner's tax return will include a Self-Employment section in which Standard Accounts Information is entered in the form of a Profit and Loss Account and a Balance Sheet. The format of the Standard Accounts Information is the same for each taxpayer irrespective of the trade or profession being carried on.

For practitioners in a partnership their individual tax returns include a Partnership section in which their share of partnership income is entered. The Standard Accounts Information is not entered on the individual's return but on the Partnership return.

Self Assessment and Partnerships

Each year a partnership must file a completed Partnership Tax Return. This return shows the Standard Accounts Information. It must contain all the income and expenses relating to the partnership including partners' individual expenses even though these may not appear in the partnership accounts. Individual partners can no longer make separate expenses claims for payments made outside the partnership (e.g. use of home; spouse's salary; motor expenses). It is the responsibility of a designated partner to make the return although all partners are responsible for its content.

There is no longer any partnership tax liability and the Partnership Tax return will only show the amounts of profit and other income allocated to each partner. These amounts are then entered in each partner's individual tax return and each will calculate their own liability and be responsible for paying their own tax.

The East Road Surgery

Refer to chapter 5, Presentation of the Financial Statements, Profit and Loss Account shows the partnership practice has made a total net profit of £155602 for the year ended 31 March 1998.

The partnership agreement required profits to be shared equally but each partner was entitled to an adjustment for any expenditure incurred on behalf of the partnership.

The partners withdrew cash in equal amounts to pay (i) for the maintenance of their cars and (ii) use of home as office. Hire purchase interest on cars was also paid by the practice.

The profit to be divided between partners as adjusted for tax purposes as follows:-

Profit per Accounts Y.E. 31.3.1998		£
		155602
Add back:	Depreciation	20695
	Motor Expenses	9000
	Use of Home	1200
	HP Interest on Cars	7200

		193697
Less:	Bank Interest Received	(1500)
	Capital Allowances	(7471)

Profit to be shared before individual adjustments		184726

East Road Surgery refurbished its premises during the year ended 31 March 1997. No capital allowances could be claimed on such improvements. The practice did look into the 'cost rent scheme' but it was not possible because of the HA's restrictions. The practice was already on a 'Notional Rent' scheme and the only option available was for an improvement grant.

The practice also received grants under the GP Computer scheme. Here, the net cost of the capital assets are reported in the practice accounts. Capital allowances are claimed on the net capital costs.

The East Road Surgery

Capital Allowances Computation 1997/98

	Pool £	CA £
Written down value b/fwd	29884	
Writing down allowance 25%	(7471)	7471
	---------	---------
Written down value c/fwd	22413	

Motor Cars

Capital Allowances which are due, based on separate pools and adjusted for private usage, is as follows:-

	Dr Brayne £	CA £
Addition 6.4.97	17640	
Writing down allowance	(3000) x 80%*	2400
	---------	---------
	14640	

	Dr Drane £	CA £
Addition 6.4.97	17640	
Writing down allowance	(3000) x 75%*	2250
	---------	---------
	14640	

	Dr Payne £	CA £
Addition 6.4.97	17640	
Writing down allowance	(3000) x 85%*	2550
	---------	---------
	14640	

Notes: For private cars costing more than £12000 the writing down allowance is restricted to £3000 per annum.

   CA = Capital Allowances
*The 'business use' percentages are based on each GP's mileage log record.

The East Road Surgery

Expenditures incurred by individual partners after adjusting for private usage is as follows:-

	Dr Brayne £	Dr Drane £	Dr Payne £
Motor Expenses	2875	2750	2950
Business Use of Home	575	450	350

HP interest is adjusted in the same proportion as the capital allowances:

	£1920	£1800	£2040

Allocation of Profit between partners:

		Total £	Dr Brayne £	Dr Drane £	Dr Payne £
Profit before individual adjustments		184726	62167	62167	60392*
Less:	Motor Exp.	(8575)	(2875)	(2750)	(2950)
	Use of Home	(1375)	(575)	(450)	(350)
	HP Interest	(5760)	(1920)	(1800)	(2040)
	Capital Allow.	(7200)	(2400)	(2250)	(2550)
Net Share of Taxable Profits		161816	54397	54917	52502

Bank interest received is taxed separately on each partner according to his or her share.

	Total	Dr Brayne	Dr Drane	Dr Payne
Bank interest received (gross)	£1500	£500	£500	£500

*Profit share: Dr Payne's share was 51/52 x £184,726 / 3.

In the case study, partners have agreed to pay their individual tax liabilities from their normal drawings.

Appendix A

Summary of Tax Rates & Allowances

Summary of Tax Rates & Allowances

Rates: **1998/99**				**1997/98**			
Taxable Income	Band	Rate	Tax	Taxable Income	Band	Rate	Tax
£	£	%	£	£	£	%	£
1 - 4300	4300	20	860	1 - 4100	4100	20	820
4301 - 27100	22800	23	5244	4101 - 26100	22000	23	5820
27101 Upwards		40		26101 Upwards		40	

Personal Allowances:	**1998/99**	**1997/98**
	£	£
Personal allowance	4195	4045
Age 65 - 74	5410	5220
Age 75 and over	5600	5400
Married couple allowance*	1900	1830
Age 65 - 74	3305	3185
Age 75 and over	3345	3225
Where the income less charges exceeds....	16200	15600

age-related allowances are reduced by
50% of the excess until the basic personal
allowance becomes more beneficial.

Additional allowance for children*	1900	1830
Wife's bereavement allowance*	1900	1830

*Relief only at 15% rate.
Relief reduced to 10% in 1999/2000.

National Insurance Class 4

6% of profits between	7310 - 25220	7010 - 4180
Max. NIC Class 4 payable	1074.60	1030.20
From 1996/97 the 50% deduction is abolished.		
NIC Class 2 Weekly rate	6.35	6.15

Superannuation Contribution:

Basic contributions	6%	6%

Erratum

Partly superannuable income proportions used:

Accounts year to 31.3.1998	69.1%
The correct percentage should have been	66.4%
Budget forecast to 31.3.1999	65.5%

Check with your professional advisors.

Summary of Tax Rates & Tables (ctd):

Capital Allowances   First Year Allowance

Expenditure between
2 July 1997 to1 July 1998   50%
2 July 1998 to1 July 1999   40%

Writing Down Allowance rate is 25%.

	1998/99	1997/98
	£	£
PAYE thresholds - Weekly	80.50	78.00
Monthly	350.00	338.00
NIC thresholds - Weekly	64.00	62.00
Monthly	278.00	260.00
Capital Gain Tax	£	£
Annual exemption limit	6800	6500
Tapered Gains:		
From 5/4/1998, indexation of gains has been abolished and in its place a system of tapered relief is introduced.		
Retirement Relief 100% relief for gains up to	250000	250000
50% relief for gains up to	1000000	1000000
VAT	from 1.4.98	from 1.12.97
Standard rate	17.5%	17.5%
	£	£
Registration Limit	50000	49000
De-registration limit	48000	47000

Inheritance Tax

	On or after	
	6.4.98	6.4.97
	£	£
Gross cumulative transfer	0 - 223000	0 - 215000
Tax rate - transfer on death	Nil	Nil
lifetime transfer	Nil	Nil
Gross cumulative transfer	223000 upwards	215000 upwards
Tax rate - transfer on death	40%	40%
lifetime transfer	20%	20%

Appendix B

SUMMARY
OF
FEES
&
ALLOWANCES
PAYABLE
TO
GPs

Source: NHS Executive/The Red Book

	From 1 Dec 98 £	From 1 Apr 98 £	From 1 Apr 97 £
PRACTICE ALLOWANCES			

Basic Practice Allowance: SFA Para 12

Full time Practitioners:

A practitioner will be eligible for the maximum rate of BPA if he provides general medical services and has 1,200 or more patients on his personal list, or if he is a member of a partnership, the average list is at least 1,200 patients for each practitioner.

	From 1 Dec 98 £	From 1 Apr 98 £	From 1 Apr 97 £
Full time practitioner provides services for at least 26 hours a week.	7,776	7,584	7,488

Part time Practitioners:

.A practitioner will be eligible for a lower rate iif he has at least 400 but no more than 1,199]patients on the list. Payments will be made on (the following basis:

No	1998 Dec @ £	1998 Apr @ £	1997 Apr @ £	From 1 Dec 98 £	From 1 Apr 98 £	From 1 Apr 97 £
400				3,240	3,160	3,120
200	8.10	7.90	7.80	1,620	1,580	1,560
200	6.48	6.32	6.24	1,296	1,264	1,248
200	4.86	4.74	4.68	972	948	936
200	3.24	3.16	3.12	648	632	624
-------				--------	--------	--------
1200				7,776	7,584	7,488

	From 1 Dec 98 £	From 1 Apr 98 £	From 1 Apr 97 £
¾ Time practitioner provides services for 19 to 26 hours a week.	6,642	6,478	6,396
½ Time practitioner provides services for at least 13 hours a week.	4,860	4,740	4,680

Note: Practitioner means unrestricted principal; it could be full time, part-time or job sharing unrestricted principal.

	From 1 Dec 98 £	From 1 Apr 98 £	From 1 Apr 97 £
Job sharers:			

Two practitioners, who together provide general medical services for at least 26 hours per week, are treated jointly as a single practitioner.

The difference between a job sharer and a part time GP:

Job sharers are jointly eligible for a single basic practice allowance at the appropriate rate, calculated both in accordance with their combined list sizes, irrespective of their personal list sizes, and with the average list size where they are members of a partnership.

Calculating partnership average list size:

For example, with a partnership of 2 full time and one half time practitioner the devisor will be 2.5; in a partnership of 3 full time, one three-quarter and one half time will be 4.25.

Example 1:

	BPA Patients No	Entitlement No	BPA	BPA	BPA
F/time	1,000	1,200	7,776	7,584	7,488
F/time	1,300	1,200	7,776	7,584	7,488
½ time	700	600	4,860	4,740	4,680
	--------	--------			
	3,000 / 2.5				

Example 2:

	BPA Patients No	Entitlement No	BPA	BPA	BPA
F/time	1,400	1,280	7,776	7,584	7,488
F/time	1,300	1,280	7,776	7,584	7,488
F/time	1,200	1,280	7,776	7,584	7,488
¾ time	840	900	6,642	6,478	6,396
½ time	700	700	4,860	4,740	4,680
	--------	--------			
	5,440 / 4.25				

	From 1 Dec 98 £	From 1 Apr 98 £	From 1 Apr 97 £
Leave Payment (leave advance):			
20% of BPA	1,555	1,517	1,496

Part of the total basic practice allowance expected to be payable for a financial year maybe drawn as a 'leave payment' at the time a period of holiday or study leave is taken. The practitioner should submit a claim by 15 April each year and he will be entitled to an advance of 20% BPA. Any payment made will be repayable by equal quarterly instalments so that the whole of the amount is recovered by 31 March in the year following the advance.

Additions to the BPA - SFA Para 13

In respect of:

(a)   Practice in designated area
(b)   Seniority
(c)   Employment of an Assistant (full time)

The rate below will be paid to a Practitioner receiving the maximum rate of BPA. Those who are not eligible for the maximum rate of BPA will be paid proportionally, as follows:-

$$\frac{\text{BPA received}}{\text{Max. rate of BPA}}$$

Practices in Designated Area - SFA Para 14

A very few number of GPs are receiving payments for practicing in a designated area.

Type 1 Allowance	3,775	3,705	3,645

is payable to a practitioner whose main surgery is in an area, which has been designated continuously for at least 3 years. The allowance will continue for a concessionary period of 3 years after the area ceases to be designated.

	From 1 Dec 98 £	From 1 Apr 98 £	From 1 Apr 97 £
Type 2 Allowance	5,760	5,650	5,560

is payable to a practitioner whose own main surgery is in an area, whch has, been continuously designated for 1 year with average lists of 3,000 or more patients. The allowance continues for a concessionary period of 2 years after the average drops below' 3,000

Seniority Allowance - SFA Para 16

Payment for seniority will be made to every practitioner eligible for a basic practice allowance:

1st level payment to a practitioner who has been registered for 11 years or more and has been providing services for at least 7 years.	480	470	465
2nd level payment to a practitioner who has been registered for 18 years or more and has been providing services for at least 14 years.	2,510	2,465	2,425
3rd level payment to a practitioner who has been registered for 25 years or more and has been providing services for at least 21 years.	5,425	5,320	5,235

Employment of an Assistant - SFA Para 18

Full time assistant:

Normal	6,750	6,620	6,515
Designated Area	9,450	9,270	9,120

An allowance will be paid in respect of the employment of a full time assistant to:

(i)   a single handed full time GP or 2 job sharers with a list of at least 3,000 patients; or

(ii)   a partnership of full time GPs with at least 3,000 patients for the first full time GP or 2 job sharers plus an average of 2,500 patients for each other full time GP or set of 2 job sharers; or

(iii)   a partnership of at least 1 full time GP or 2 job sharers plus one or more part time GPs with a minimum combined list of 3,000 patients for the first full time GP or 2 job sharers, 2,500 for each other full time GP or set of 2 job sharers; 1,250 patients for each $\frac{1}{2}$ time GPs and 1,875 patients for each $\frac{3}{4}$ time GPs.

Less than full time assistant:

An allowance of half the appropriate rate will be paid in respect of the employment of an assistant working half time or more to:

(i)   as above, with a list size of at least 2,500 patients; or

     Rural areas:
     at least 1,000 patients

(ii)   as above, substitute 2,500 and 2,250 patients respectively; or

     Rural areas:
     at least 1,000 patients per partner or 2 job sharers.

(iii)   as above, substitute 2,500, 2,250, 1,125 and 1,687 patients; or Rural areas:

     at least 1,000 patients per GP or 2 job sharers, 500 patients per $\frac{1}{2}$ time GP or 750 per $\frac{3}{4}$ time GP.

	From	From	From
	1 Dec 98	1 Apr 98	1 Apr 97
	£	£	£

Associate Allowance - SFA Para 19

A single-handed GP or job sharing GP must be:

(i) in receipt of rural practice payments

(ii) sole GP on an island

(iii) in receipt of an inducement payment

(iv) >10 miles from main surgery and General Hospital.

	From 1 Dec 98 £	From 1 Apr 98 £	From 1 Apr 97 £
1st year	27,310	26,735	26,120
2nd year	28,690	28,085	27,440
3rd year	30,070	29,435	28,760
4th and subsequent years	31,450	30,785	30,080

SFA Para 19.19

An associate will be eligible to receive the PGE allowance according to the above criteria. A responsible GP should make the claim on behalf of the associate and it will be a condition of payment of this allowance that the responsible GP pays the full amount to the associate.

153

	From 1 Dec 98 £	From 1 Apr 98 £	From 1 Apr 97 £
Post Graduate Education Allowance - SFA Para 37			
A practitioner will be paid an allowance	2,445	2,400	2,360

if (i) he has attended 25 days of post graduate education over 5 years preceding the claim; and

  (ii) he has attended at least 2 courses in each of the following 3 subject areas:

    Health Promotion/Prevention of Illness
    Disease Management
    Service Management

Each partner in a job sharing arrangement will be eligible individually for the full allowance, if he individually satisfies the appropriate conditions.

Practitioners who fail to maintain a 5-year programme will qualify for the reduced allowance if the following conditions are met:

Level 1: He has attended at least 5 days of courses a year over the past 5 years.	490	480	470
Level 2: He has attended at least 10 days of courses a year over the past 5 years - including at least 1 course in each of the 2 subject areas.	980	960	940
Level 3: He has attended at least 15 days of courses a year over the past 5 years - including at least 1 course in each of the 3 subject areas.	1,470	1,440	1,410
Level 4: He has attended at least 20 days of courses a year over the past 5 years - including at least 1 course in each of the 3 subject areas.	1,960	1,920	1,880

CAPITATION FEES	From 1 Dec 98 £	From 1 Apr 98 £	From 1 Apr 97 £

Standard Capitation Fees - SFA Para 21

Capitation fees will be paid in respect of patients on the personal list of a GP. Payments will be made at the 3 rates based on the ages of patients on the last day of the preceding quarter.

For patients aged:

Under 65	16.65	16.30	16.05
65 - 74	21.95	21.55	21.20
75 and over	42.50	41.65	41.00

Capitation Addition - SFA Para 82

Out of Hours	3.45	3.25	3.20

Payable to doctors who provide cover for GPs relieved of responsibility of out of hours duties.

Deprivation Fee - SFA Para 20

A practitioner providing services to a patient who is resident in a deprived area, will be eligible to receive a Deprivation Fee. The payments are made at 3 levels in accordance with the degree of deprivation of the area in which the patient lives:

A high level of deprivation	11.60	11.40	11.20
A medium level of deprivation	8.70	8.55	8.40
A low level of deprivation	6.70	6.55	6.45

	From 1 Dec 98 £	From 1 Apr 98 £	From 1 Apr 97 £
Registration Fee - SFA Para 23			
A practitioner will be eligible for a Registration Fee for all new registrations except for:			
(i) a child under 5 years old and			
(ii) a patient of a partner who during 12 months prior to the date of acceptance participated in a consultation.	7.35	7.20	7.10
Child Health Surveillance Fee - SFA Para 22			
A practitioner who wishes to provide Child Health Surveillance and receive a fee for such services must apply to the HA for inclusion in the CHS list. A capitation supplement is received for each child under 5 years old registered with him for the purposes of CHS.	12.05	11.85	11.65

	From 1 Dec 98 £	From 1 Apr 98 £	From 1 Apr 97 £

TARGET PAYMENTS

Childhood Immunisation - SFA Para 25
Aged 2 and under

Maximum sum payable to a practitioner in a partnership with an average of 22 children aged 2 per GP.

Higher Rate target payment:

	From 1 Dec 98	From 1 Apr 98	From 1 Apr 97
90% of the number of courses need to achieve full immunisation.	2,430	2,370	2,340
Lower Rate target payment:			
70% of the number of courses needed to achieve full immunisation.	810	790	780

Definition of age 2 groups:

are those born between the 2nd day of the same quarter 3 years earlier, and the 1st quarter of the corresponding quarter one year later inclusive.

For example, on 1.10.1999 (1998) the target population of children includes those born between 2.10.1996 (1995) and 1.10.1997 (1996)

Definition of complete courses of immunisation (aged 2):

Group 1 DTP   3 doses
Group 2 P   3 doses
Group 3 MMR   1 dose
Group 4 Hib   3 doses
or a single dose after age 13 months.

Maximum sum payable:

No of aged 2 on   Max sum payable
partnership list   to average GP
------------------------- x
22 x No. of partners

For example, 3 partners practice has 60 children aged 2 on the list. All completed courses of immunisation in Group 1 of which 30 complete immunisation given by the GP's own partnership, 15 by another GP and 15 by Health Authority.

45 of the children have had complete course of immunisation in Group 2. Of these 24 were given by GP's own partnership, 21 by a HA Clinic.

36 of the children have had complete courses of immunisation in Group 3. Of these 15 were given by the GP's own partnership, 6 by another GP, and 15 by a HA Clinic.

54 of the children had had complete courses of immunisation in Group 4. Of these 30 were given by the GP's own partnership, 4 by another GP and 20 by a HA Clinic.

How many completing immunisations are needed to reach the target?

Step 1: 60 children x 4 Groups =

240 max. completing immunisation

70% target requires 168 completing immunisation.

90% target requires 216 completing immunisation.

Step 2: Has the target been reached?

Group 1	60)	70%
Group 2	45)	target
Group 3	36)	has been
Group 4	54)	reached

	195	

Step 3: What is the maximum sum payable?

The National average for one GP's list is 22 children. Here, the maximum annual target payment is lower rate due to 70% target reached and then divide by 4 to give quarterly rate.

Partnership list

------------------------- x £ rate

22 x No. of partners

Based on above example   Max Payable

Dec 1998 Rate	£184.10
Apr 1998 Rate	£179.55
Apr 1997 Rate	£177.27

Step 4: What proportion of the work needed to reach the target was done by all practices as part of GMS?

Group 1: This practice   30)
          Other GP   15) 45

Since 70% = 42, 42 > 30, so take 42.

Group 2: This practice   24)
          Other GP   Nil) 24

Since 70% = 17, 17 < 24, so take 24.

Group 3: This practice   15)
          Other GP   6) 21

Since 70% = 15, 15 = 15, so take 21.

```
Group 4: This practice    30
        Other GP           4
                         ----
                          34
                         ----
```

Since 70% = 24, 24 < 30, so take 34.

```
So, total of these =  G1        42
                      G2        24
                      G3        21
                      G4        34
                              -----
No. of doses given by GPs      121
                              -----

No. needed to reach 70%        168
                              -----
```

GMS proportion = 121/168 = 72%

Step 5:   How much is the payment?

Max. payment x GMS
proportion

Based on this example, each partner
receives:

Dec 1998 Rate   £132.60

Apr 1998 Rate   £129.32

Apr 1997 Rate   £127.68

Based on above example, total
payment to partnership is:

```
Dec 1998 Rate    £132.60 x 3 = £397.80
                              ----------

Apr 1998 Rate    £129.32 x 3 = £387.96
                              ----------

Apr 1997 Rate    £127.68 x 3 = £383.04
                              ----------
```

	From 1 Dec 98 £	From 1 Apr 98 £	From 1 Apr 97 £
Pre School Boosters - SFA Para 26			

Maximum sum payable to a practitioner in a partnership with an average of 22 children aged 5 per GP.

A GP will be eligible for a full target payment if on the first day of a quarter 90% of the children on the partnership list who are aged 5 have had reinforcing doses of DT and P immunisation.

	From 1 Dec 98 £	From 1 Apr 98 £	From 1 Apr 97 £
	720	705	690

A GP will be eligible for a lower level of payment if 70% of these children have had such reinforcing doses.

	240	235	230

Max. sum payable =

No. of children aged 5
on a partnership list   Max. sum
----------------------   x   payable
22 x No. of partners   to an
                              average GP

where 22 is the no. of children aged 5 on the list of average GP.

Example:

On the first day of the quarter, a 3 partners practice has 67 children aged 5 on its list. Of these 50 have had pre school boosters, 49 of which were given by GPs as part of GMS.

Step 1: Has the target been reached? If so, which?

No. of boosters needed to reach targets:

90% target = 0.9 x 67 = 60
70% target = 0.7 x 67 = 47

therefore, 70% target has been reached.

Step 2: What is the max. payable?

No. of children aged 5
on the partners' list
-------------------------- x
22 x No. of partners

Lower target
payment
per quarter

Based on above   Max. Payable
example

Dec 1998 Rate   £60.91

Apr 1998 Rate   £59.64

Apr 1997 Rate   £58.37

Step 3: How much of the work needed to reach the target was done by GP as part of GMS?

No. given by such practitioners = 49

No. given to reach 70%   = 47

This is limited to 100% or 47/47 in order that no more than the max. payment is made.

Step 4: How much is the payment?

Max. payment x GMS proportion

Based on this example, each partner receives:

Dec 1998 Rate   £60.91
Apr 1998 Rate   £59.64
Apr 1997 Rate   £58.37

Based on above example, total payment to partnership is:

Dec 1998 Rate   £60.91 x 3 = £182.73

Apr 1998 Rate   £59.64 x 3 = £178.92

Apr 1997 Rate   £58.37 x 3 = £175.11

	From 1 Dec 98 £	From 1 Apr 98 £	From 1 Apr 97 £

Cervical Cytology - SFA Para 28

A GP will be eligible for payment if on the first day of a quarter 80% of the eligible women on the partnership list who are aged 25 to 64 have had an adequate cervical smear test, taken by any source, during the 5.5 years preceding the claim. A GP will be eligible for a lower payment if the level is 50%.

Maximum sums payable to a GP in a partnership with an average of 430 eligible women aged 25 to 64 per practitioner.

	From 1 Dec 98 £	From 1 Apr 98 £	From 1 Apr 97 £
Higher payment	2,700	2,655	2,610
Lower payment	900	885	870

The max sum payable is therefore:

No. of eligible women
aged 25 to 64 on the   Max. sum
partners' list   payable to
-------------------------- x average GP
430 x No. of partners

where 430 is the no. of eligible women on the average GP list.

Exclude women who do not have a cervix.

Example:

On the first day of the quarter a 4 partners practice has 2,130 women aged 25 to 64 on its list. Of these, 1,680 have had adequate cervical smear tests during the 5.5 years preceding the claim of which 1,400 were taken by GPs as part of the GM Services. 44 of the women aged 25 to 64 on the list do not have a cervix and of these, 23 have had an adequate cervical smear test in the relevant period.

Step 1: How many adequate smears are needed to reach the target?

80% target = 0.8 x (2,130 - 44)
= 1,669

50% target = 0.5 x (2,130 - 44)
= 1,043

Step 2: How the target has been reached?

Total no. of smears taken less the no taken from those who do not have a cervix.

1,680 - 23 = 1,657

The 50% target has been reached.

Step 3: What is the max. payable?

No. of eligible women on partners' list		Lower target
--------------------------	x	payment
430 x no. of partners		per quarter

Based on above example   Max. Payable

Dec 1998 Rate	£272.88
Apr 1998 Rate	£268.33
Apr 1997 Rate	£263.78

Step 4: How much, of the work needed to reach the target, was done by GPs as part of GMS?

No. given by such practitioners = 1,400

No. needed to reach 50% = 1,043

$$\text{GMS Prop} = \frac{1,400}{1,043}$$

This is limited to 100% or 1,043/1,043 in order that no more than the maximum payment is made.

Step 5: How much is the payment?

Max. payment x GMS prop.

Based on above example, each partner receives:

Dec 1998 Rate	£272.88
Apr 1998 Rate	£268.33
Apr 1997 Rate	£263.78

Based on above example, total
payment to partnership is:

Dec 1998 Rate	£272.88 x 4 = £1,091.52
Apr 1998 Rate	£268.33 x 4 = £1,073.32
Apr 1997 Rate	£263.78 x 4 = £1,055.12

	From 1 Dec 98 £	From 1 Apr 98 £	From 1 Apr 97 £

HEALTH PROMOTION ACTIVITIES & CHRONIC DISEASE MANAGEMENT

GPs will be eligible for payment for participating in HP Activities and CDMP.

Health Promotion Activities: - SFA Para 30

Practitioners will be able to claim fees for such activities as well-person, anti-smoking, alcohol control, dietary control and so on, subject to approval by HA.

Annual payment for a GP with 1,884 patients	2,340	2,295	2,260

(Adjusted pro rata for other list sizes)

Chronic Disease Management
Programme - SFA Para 30

Care of patients with diabetes or asthma generally qualified for payments subject to approval by HA.

Diabetes Allowance	410	400	395
Asthma Allowance	410	400	395

	From 1 Dec 98 £	From 1 Apr 98 £	From 1 Apr 97 £

SESSIONAL PAYMENTS

Minor Surgery - SFA Para 42

The fee for minor surgery will be payable to a GP on a Health Authority's Minor Surgery List who provides a minor surgery session.

	From 1 Dec 98	From 1 Apr 98	From 1 Apr 97
	121.00	118.65	116.80

A GP will be eligible for no more than 3 such payments in respect of any quarter.

In a partnership, a GP may claim a higher number of payments but it shall not exceed 3 times the number of partners in respect of any one quarter.

	From 1 Dec 98 £	From 1 Apr 98 £	From 1 Apr 97 £

ITEM OF SERVICE FEE

(i) A fee for an item of service carried out for reason of public policy -
Vaccination and Immunisation
- SFA Para 27

A type doses	4.05	3.95	3.90
B type doses	5.85	5.75	5.65

Where:

A is a first and second dose
B is final and/or reinforcing dose

(Diphtheria/Tetanus/Polio/Smallpox/
Measles/Rubella/Anthrax/ Typhoid/
Hepatitis and Haemophilus)

(ii) **Contraceptive - SFA Para 29**

There are 2 levels of fees

(a) the ordinary fee is payable when the GP accepts a patient, gives advice and conducts any necessary examination, where appropriate prescribes drugs or an occlusive cap and follow up care.	15.45	15.15	14.90
(b) intrauterine device fee per year is payable to a GP who inserts the device and gives any necessary after care needed in the ensuing 12 months.	51.60	50.60	49.80
1st quarter	39.90	39.20	38.50
2nd quarter	3.90	3.80	3.70
3rd quarter	3.90	3.80	3.70
4th quarter	3.90	3.80	3.70

		From 1 Dec 98 £	From 1 Apr 98 £	From 1 Apr 97 £
(iii)	**Temporary Resident Fee - SFA Para 32**			
	A GP who treats a temporary resident who remains in the district for			
	< 15 days will be paid a fee of	9.80	9.60	9.45
	16 days or more will be paid a fee of	14.70	14.40	14.20
(iv)	**Arrest of Dental Haemorrhage - SFA Para 35**			
	or the provision of after care	24.45	24.00	23.60
	Fee for removal of plugs and/or stitches only	16.70	16.35	16.10
(v)	**Emergency Treatment Fees - SFA Para 33**			

When a GP on the medical list of an HA is called upon to provide treatment in the locality of the HA, in the case of an accident or other emergency for a person not on his own list or that of a partner shall be paid a fee.

(a)	Emergency Consultation:			
(1)	Involving a night visit	22.45	22.00	21.65
(2)	Other Consultation	24.45	24.00	23.60
(b)	Minor surgical operation involving local or general anaesthetic	*24.45	24.00	23.60
(c)	Treatment of fracture	*24.45	24.00	23.60
(d)	Reduction of a dislocation	*24.45	24.00	23.60
(e)	Administration of a general anaesthetic	*40.75	40.00	39.35

*A night visit fee may be paid as well.

	From 1 Dec 98 £	From 1 Apr 98 £	From 1 Apr 97 £
(vi) **2nd GP is required - SFA Para 34**			
to provide the services for the purpose of general anaesthetic	40.75	40.00	39.35
A night consultation fee may be paid as well as a fee under (b) to (e) as appropriate			
(vii) **Immediately Necessary Treatment - SFA Para 36**			
A GP who gives any immediately necessary treatment to a person whom he refused to accept for inclusion on his list or as a temporary resident, will be paid a fee. Up to 15 days	9.80	9.60	9.45
16 days or more	14.70	14.40	14.20
(viii) **Night Payments - SFA Para 24**			
providing out of hours services (between 10pm and 8am)	2,245	2,200	2,165
All GPs in general medical practice will be eligible for the annual payment. Job sharers providing such services shall jointly be eligible for a single annual payment.			
Consultation fee	22.45	22.00	21.65
A GP is paid a fee for each consultation for services rendered during out of hour to patient who is on his list or a temporary resident or a woman for whom he has undertaken to provide MMS.			

	From 1 Dec 98 £	From 1 Apr 98 £	From 1 Apr 97 £
(ix) Maternity Medical Services - SFA Para 31			
(a) Complete Maternity Medical Services fees:			
15A - GP on Obstetrics list is paid higher rate.			
15B - GP not on Obstetrics list is paid lower rate.			
Where a full Maternity Medical Service (MMS) is provided, a GP qualifies for a lower fee.	112.60	110.25	108.50
Where a comprehensive service during pregnancy of a patient, includes the confinement and post natal period, is provided, a GP qualifies for higher fee	193.00	189.00	186.00
(b) Ante-natal Care fees:			
Where the patient is confined after the 24th week (or earlier where the live birth results) one of the three levels of fees are payable for ante- natal care			
Women pregnancy booking - Up to 16th week Lower fee	60.80	59.55	58.60
Higher fee	104.20	102.05	100.40
17th to 30th week Lower fee	45.60	44.65	43.95
Higher fee	78.15	76.55	75.35
From 31st week Lower fee	30.40	29.75	29.30
Higher fee	52.10	51.05	50.20

	From 1 Dec 98 £	From 1 Apr 98 £	From 1 Apr 97 £

(c) Miscarriage Fee:

If a patient who has not made
arrangements for MMS requires
treatment for a miscarriage before
the 8th week of pregnancy, her own
GP should attend her as part of the
GMS. In other cases where the
pregnancy ends in or before the 24th
week and does not result in a live
birth the miscarriage fee is payable
for MMS to the patient.

Lower fee	40.20	39.40	38.75
Higher fee	64.35	63.00	62.00

(d) Care during Confinement Fee:

The fee is payable to a GP who
provides MMS during a
confinement including cases where
the GP is called during labour to a
patient who is not booked for MMS
with a GP.

Lower fee	25.75	25.20	24.80
Higher fee	44.40	43.45	42.80

(e) Post-natal Care:

The complete post-natal care fee is
payable to a GP who provides MMS
to mother and child throughout the
14 days immediately after
confinement and carries out a full
post-natal examination at or about 6
weeks after confinement and in any
event not later than 12 weeks thereafter.

Lower fee	31.50	30.85	30.35
Higher fee	44.40	43.45	42.80

	From 1 Dec 98 £	From 1 Apr 98 £	From 1 Apr 97 £
(f) Partial post-natal care:			

A fee for partial post-natal care is payable for each attendance to give medical care to either the mother or her child during the 14 days after the confinement.

Lower fee	4.15	4.05	4.00
Maximum	20.75	20.25	19.75
Higher fee	5.90	5.80	5.70
Maximum	29.50	29.00	28.50

Full post-natal examination:

A separate fee is payable for full post-natal examination.

Lower fee	10.75	10.60	10.25
Higher fee	14.90	14.45	14.30

| Fee for 2nd GP giving anaesthetic additional fee is payable to the GP providing the MMS. | 40.75 | 40.00 | 37.50 |

	From 1 Dec 98 £	From 1 Apr 98 £	From 1 Apr 97 £
PAYMENTS IN RESPECT OF GP REGISTRAR SCHEME - SFA Para 38			
(a) Training Grant	5,325	5,220	5,140
(b) Allowance for additional motor vehicle -			
(i) for 1 year's full time training	3,928	3,928	3,928
(ii) for 2 year's part time training (for each year)	2,569	2,569	2,569
(c) GP Registrar's salary and supplement			
1st year senior	31,765	31,095	
2nd year senior	33,455	32,750	
3rd year senior	35,145	34,405	
4th year senior	36,835	36,060	
5th year senior	38,525	37,710	
6th year senior	40,215	39,365	
(d) London Weighting:			
(i) London Zone	1,543	1,543	1,543
(ii) The Fringe Zone	149	149	149
(e) GP Registrar subscription to a professional defence organisation.			
RURAL PRACTICE PAYMENTS - SFA Para 43			
Unit Value	0.219	0.219	0.219
DOCTORS' RETAINER SCHEME - SFA Para 39			

Clinical tutors will arrange for doctors in the Scheme to do service sessions in general practice where the doctor so wishes and the clinical tutor agrees. Payment will be made by the HA up to a maximum of the appropriate fee for a notional half day per week to GPs who employ a member of the scheme as an assistant.

Fee per session is	47.75	45.75	44.10

	From 1 Dec 98 £	From 1 Apr 98 £	From 1 Apr 97 £
ADDITIONAL PAYMENT DURING SICKNESS/CONFINEMENT - SFA Para 48-49			
Weekly maximum	474.80	464.80	448.00
PROLONGED STUDY LEAVE - SFA Para 50			
Educational Allowance	66.95	65.50	63.15
Locum allowance a max.	474.80	464.80	454.00
INITIAL PRACTICE ALLOWANCES - SFA Para 41			
Type 1 for Single Handed Practices in designated areas:			
1st year	24,300	23,550	23,010
2nd year	16,200	15,700	15,340
3rd year	8,100	7,850	7,670
4th year	4,050	3,925	3,835
Amount to be compared with Total Reckonable Income in previous years	25,940	25,940	25,940

Small single handed practice is one in which the annual income from capitation & allowances could fall short of the allowance in the 1st year to a GP setting up a new practice.

Type 2 for Practices in Special areas:

1st Doctor guaranteed net	63,740	61,800	60,385
2nd Doctor jointly guaranteed net	112,770	109,340	106,835

Areas of major housing development where considerable population increase in a comparatively few years is expected, and where it is desirable to have, at the outset, full time GP of experience and personal qualities to establish general practice.

	From 1 Dec 98 £	From 1 Apr 98 £	From 1 Apr 97 £
PAYMENTS TO GPs PROVIDING TEMP COVER - SFA Para 46			
Max. annual rate 75% of IANI	36,770	25,655	34,840
LOCUM ALLOWANCE - SFA Para 47			
For single handed in rural areas attending courses	474.80	464.80	454.00

LONDON INITIATIVE ZONE - SFA Para 57

Workforce Flexibilities:

Scheme ends on 31.3.98

Type 3	LIZ Initial Practice Allowance	10,000
	LIZ Collaborative Working Allowance	5,000
	LIZ Associate Doctor Scheme	7,500
	LIZ Assistant Scheme	15,000

DRUGS OR APPLIANCES - SFA Para 44 & Sch 1-6

(i)   The basic price less any discount calculated in accordance with paragraph 44/schedule 1;

(ii) an on-cost allowance of 10.5% of the basic price before deduction of any discount under paragraph 44/schedule 1;

(iii) a container allowance of 3.8p per prescription;

(iv) a dispensing fee as shown in paragraph 44/schedule 2;

(v)   an allowance in respect of VAT calculated in accordance with paragraph 44.4;

(vi) exceptional expenses as provided for in Part II Clause 12 of the Drug Tariff.

INDUCEMENTS - SFA Para 45

An inducement payment will be available for a full time GP practicing in an area where the HA has accepted that it is essential to maintain a medical practice though the area is unattractive to a GP.

RENT & RATES SCHEME
- SFA Para 51

All GPs will be eligible to receive payment under this scheme, except where a GP has less than 100 patients on his list. In this case he has to satisfy the HA that he is in the process of building up his practice.

Reimbursements of rent and rates by HA's will be calculated on the basis described as follows:

Rents:
(a)   Cost rents for new separate purpose built premises or their equivalent

(b)   Notional rents for owner occupiers in respect of separate premises and in respect of surgeries in residences.

(c)   Payments for - rented separate premises
                  - premises in rented residences
                  - premises rented from local authorities where they charge an economic rent

(d)   Any rent or accomodation charge for premises incurred by practitioners who occupy a health centre under any tenancy or under licence granted by a NHS Trust.

Rates:
For all forms of rent reimbursements, the appropriate business rate together with rates

described as water, sewerage, miscellaenous or environmental rates levied by a water or sewerage undertaking will be reimbursed.

PRACTICE STAFF SCHEME
- SFA Para 52

This scheme provides for direct reimbursement, at the HA's discretion, of all or part of the expense of employing suitable practice staff.

IMPROVEMENT GRANTS
- SFA Para 56

This scheme provides for grants, at the HA's discretion, towards the cost to GPs of improving existing medical premises where prior approval of the project has been obtained from the HA.

GP COMPUTER REIMBURSEMENT
SCHEME - SFA Para 58

This scheme provides for the direct reimbursement of a proportion of the cost incurred by a GP.

	From 1 Dec 98 £	From 1 Apr 98 £	From 1 Apr 97 £
ANNUAL RATES PER DOCTORS AND DENTISTS REVIEW BODY:			
Intended Average Net Income (IANI)	49,030	47,540	46,450
Indirectly reimbursed expenses	23,400	23,400	23,200
Balancing correction	(527)	(527)	(615)
Intended Average Gross Income	71,903	70,413	69,035

Bibliography

RBDD Remuneration 27th Report 1998   HMSO

NHS GMS Statement of Fees & Allowances 1998   NHS Executive

Making Sense of the Red Book
    - Norman Ellis & John Chisholm   Radcliffe 1997

General Practitioners Handbook BMA
    - Norman Ellis   Radcliffe 1998

Practice Finance Your Questions Answered
(2nd Edition) - John Dean   Radcliffe 1998

Making Sense of Partnerships
    - Norman Ellis & Tony Stanton   Radcliffe 1994

Medical Practice Accounting & Finance
    - Rose Mary L Bukics & Donald R Chambers   R D Irwin 1995

Financial Management within GP Practices   CIMA 1992

Pocket Guide to Business Finance
    - J G Siegel, J K Shim & S W Hartman   McGraw Hill 1992

Financial Engineering
    - Jorge Gabrielczyk   Fourmat Publishing 1986

Financial Pulse Circulation   Miller Freeman

Medeconomics Circulation   Haymarket Medical Ltd

Accounting & Finance
    - Alan Pizzey   Holt, Rinehart &
       Winston Ltd 1982

Cost Accounting
    - Rod Perera   Emile Woolf
       & Associates Ltd 1980

Cost Accounting 2   LSA (ICMA & ICSA)
       Courses Ltd 1982

Cost Accounting 2   FT Publications Ltd 1982

Financial Accounting 2   Chart Foulks Lynch 1979

Self-Assessment Tax Return Guide   Inland Revenue 1997/98

Index